This book considers a variety of explanations of why political disagreement is so extensive and persistent. The author examines variants of the 'contestability' and 'imperfection' conceptions which have dominated political theory: the idea that political disagreement is so pervasive because of its value-ladenness; that key political concepts are essentially contested; that those who occupy very different political positions fail to understand each other. He argues that we need to develop a framework which borrows elements from both conceptions, presupposing some form of moral cognitivism, but recognizing that many political disputes cannot be resolved to the satisfaction of every reasonable person. Within such a framework he shows how empirical models can be constructed which give an active role not only to the agent's reasons for his or her beliefs, but also to other psychological and sociological considerations. One such model draws on Carol Gilligan's work on gender differences in moral reasoning, and Nancy Chodorow's theory of how gender is constructed.

Andrew Mason is a lecturer in the Department of Politics at the University of Hull. He was previously lecturer in moral philosophy at the University of St Andrews, and a British Academy Postdoctoral Fellow at St Peter's College, Oxford. He is the author of several articles on moral and political philosophy.

EXPLAINING POLITICAL DISAGREEMENT

EXPLAINING POLITICAL DISAGREEMENT

ANDREW MASON

CAMBRIDGE
UNIVERSITY PRESS

Published by the Press Syndicate of the University of Cambridge
The Pitt Building, Trumpington Street, Cambridge CB2 1RP
40 West 20th Street, New York, NY 10011–4211, USA
10 Stamford Road, Oakleigh, Victoria 3166, Australia

First published 1993

Printed in Great Britain at the University Press, Cambridge

A catalogue record for this book is available from the British Library

Library of Congress cataloguing in publication data
Mason, Andrew, 1959–
Explaining political disagreement/Andrew Mason.
p.   cm.
Revision of the author's thesis (doctoral).
Includes bibliographical references.
ISBN 0 521 43322 3 (hardback).
1. Consensus (Social sciences).   2. Political science – Philosophy.
I. Title.
JC328.2.M375   1993
320'.01'1–dc20   92–39228   CIP

ISBN 0 521 43322 3 hardback

CE

For my Mother
and in memory
of my Father

Contents

Preface

This book has grown out of my doctoral thesis and has benefitted greatly from the guidance I have received from a number of people. David Miller supervised the original thesis with considerable care, patience and open-mindedness; he later recommended revisions to the manuscript which gave it a clearer structure. G. A. Cohen and Russell Keat examined the thesis and provided me with invaluable comments that helped to determine the shape and content of the book it has become.

Others have been kind enough to comment upon individual chapters at various stages of development. I would like to thank Luc Bovens, Diemut Bubeck, Roger Crisp, Paul Gilbert, Jean Grimshaw, Martina Herrmann, Dan Isaacson, John Kenyon, Kristjan Kristjansson, Kathleen Lennon, Sabina Lovibond, William Lucy, Dugald Owen, Patsy Stoneman, Erik Swyngedouw, Rob Waldie, Nick Wheeler, Andrew Williams and Gavin Williams, for giving me the benefit of their judgement.

I am also grateful to the British Academy, who enabled me to spend time revising the material by awarding me one of their Postdoctoral Fellowships, and to the Master and Fellows at that time of St Peter's College, Oxford, who provided me with a congenial working environment whilst I was holding it. My final thanks are to Lynn Thomas, who I came to know towards the end of writing my thesis, and since then whose encouragement and friendship have been vital to the progress of my research.

Acknowledgements

This book incorporates revised versions of previously published articles: chapter 2 is a re-worked version of 'On Explaining Political Disagreement: the Notion of an Essentially Contested Concept', *Inquiry*, vol. 33, 1990; section 1 of chapter 3 is edited from 'Locke on Disagreement over the Use of Moral and Political Terms', *The Locke Newsletter*, no. 20, 1989; section 1 of chapter 5 is taken, with some changes, from 'Gilligan's Conception of Moral Maturity', *Journal for the Theory of Social Behaviour*, vol. 20, 1990; section 4 of chapter 5 includes paragraphs from 'Nozick on Self-Esteem', *Journal of Applied Philosophy*, vol. 7, 1990. I would like to thank the editors concerned for giving me permission to use this material again here.

Introduction

Contemporary political disagreement is extensive and persistent, and occurs at different levels of abstraction. At a practical level we are confronted by disagreement over what kinds of policies the state should pursue: for instance, whether it should enforce a sharply progressive income tax. That issue often provokes disagreement at a more theoretical level, in the form of a controversy over whether social justice requires priority to be given to the worst off through re-distributive taxation. Although many political theorists do not explicitly take a stand on the question of *why* political disagreement in its different forms resists resolution, their writings generally provide some clues as to how they would answer it were they to address it directly. The central purpose of this study is to evaluate a variety of explanations for why political disagreement is so extensive and persistent, some of which are advocated explicitly whilst others lie beneath the surface of arguments, and to develop my own account in opposition to them.

Some might doubt whether contemporary political disagreement is an important phenomenon, worthy of explanation. One strand of Marxist thought takes the view that it is insignificant on the grounds that it occurs mainly within the framework of a dominant ideology: for example, those who argue over the merits of a sharply progressive system of taxation, and over the question of whether the state should operate a redistributive taxation policy that gives priority to the needs of the worst off, generally share a commitment to a market economy in which most of the means of production are privately owned. Perhaps the forms of political disagreement which we encounter through the mass media, and indeed in academic journals, are more limited than they appear. Nevertheless different political ideologies are represented in public forums, so the idea of a dominant ideology is misleading if it encourages us to ignore the important differences between, say, 'libertarians' and social democrats, and if it fails to acknowledge the radical challenges to these viewpoints from feminist, socialist, anarchist and Green perspectives which are available, even though they are not encountered so frequently. Even if it is true that there is a dominant ideology, we should not suppose that there can be no important subordinate ideologies.

I TWO CONCEPTIONS OF POLITICAL DISAGREEMENT

Two different pictures can be distinguished each of which informs a number of accounts of why political disagreement is so pervasive and intractable. The first, which I shall call *the imperfection conception*, assumes that when political disagreement arises at least one party to the dispute is mistaken; and that with sufficient time, patience, impartiality and logical skills, political disputes could be settled to the satisfaction of any reasonable person who is sincerely engaged with them. Here the implicit idea is that disagreement is to be explained by a theory of *error*, of why some have made mistakes. A plausible theory of this kind will allow that the explanation for errors may be varied: defective reasoning, for instance, might result from a failure to take into account all the available arguments, and this in turn might be due to a lack of time or patience, or due to a partiality which motivates a selective consideration of the evidence.

The imperfection conception is committed to a form of *cognitivism* which maintains that the notion of correctness is in place in relation to moral and political thinking because when it is properly conducted it is governed by a rational method. In the history of political thought versions of the imperfection conception have been presented by theorists writing in very different social contexts. For example, in the fourteenth century Marsilius of Padua maintained that moral truths were either self-evident or could be demonstrated from truths that were self-evident. In his view the main causes of error (and hence of disagreement) were the corruption of the mind by 'nature, custom, or perverted emotion'.[1] William Godwin (1756–1836) held that moral truth can be discovered by the proper exercise of reason: when moral truths are perceived, they strike us with such force that we cannot fail to embrace them; errors arise when our

---

[1] Marsilius of Padua, *Defensor Pacis*, translated with an introduction by A. Gewirth (Toronto: University of Toronto Press, 1980), p. 7; see also p. 46.

understanding is clouded by passion and appetite.[2] John Locke
(1632–1704) was also a defender of the imperfection conception, for
he believed that moral and political disputes arise largely because
people fail to be clear in their use of terms. Locke believed that
definitions of moral terms gives us certain knowledge of their
meanings and that moral truths are open to demonstration. (He was
nevertheless pessimistic about the possibility of reaching general
agreement on moral issues because he was doubtful whether we
could get sufficiently clear on our moral and political ideas outside
of philosophical discourse.) Although it is difficult to find versions of
the imperfection conception presented explicitly today, they often
seem to be implicit, especially amongst those who are impressed by
the power of analytical philosophy but unpersuaded by the non-
cognitivist's claim that morals and politics are merely expressions of
emotion or are radically under-determined by norms of rational
inquiry in other ways.

The second picture, which I shall call *the contestability conception*,
maintains that political disagreements are intractable because
rational constraints on the proper use of political terms allow for a
variety of different applications of them: so long as there is some
measure of freedom of expression, disagreement over their proper
use will inevitably arise. The contestability conception gives no
significant role to a theory of error in explaining why political
disagreement is so intractable because it holds that in most cases
when moral and political disagreement persists, the dispute is over
which of a number of reasonable positions should be adopted, and
there is no content to the idea that any of these positions is mistaken;
there need be no failures of reasoning nor insufficient attention to
the arguments and evidence. In its crudest form, the contestability
conception has it that deep moral and political disagreements arise
as a result of differences in attitude or desire, not belief. For
example, Bertrand Russell at one time held the view that fundamental ethical disagreements, such as the disagreement between a
person who believes that all men count equally and another who
believes that one class of them alone is important, persist because the
disputants have different desires; there need be no *intellectual* error in
either of the opposing positions.[3]

[2] See M. Philp, *Godwin's Political Justice* (London: Duckworth, 1986), especially pp. 4–5.
[3] See B. Russell, 'Science and Ethics' in his *Religion and Science* (Oxford: Oxford University Press, 1935).

More sophisticated versions of the contestability conception also appear to be available. For instance, William Connolly argues that the terms of political discourse are essentially contested because 'the common resources of reason and evidence available can illuminate ... debates [over their proper use] but are insufficient to reduce the number of interpretations rationally defensible to one'.[4] Terence Ball also shows at least some sympathy for the contestability conception when he says that 'disagreement, conceptual contestation, the omnipresent threat of communicative breakdown, and the possibility of conceptual change are, as it were, built into the very structure of political discourse'.[5]

Many contemporary explanations for the extent and persistence of political disagreement do not fit neatly into one of the two conceptions I have described. The imperfection conception has several defenders in the history of moral and political thought but it is hard to find it presented explicitly and without qualification nowadays; it perhaps requires a confidence in the existence of moral truth and our ability to acquire it which is greater than many today are capable of sustaining. It is also difficult to find clear and unambiguous examples of the contestability conception, as I have described it, because it threatens to embrace a problematic form of moral relativism. Even the thesis that key political concepts are essentially contested, a version of which I have used to illustrate the contestability conception, is not a clear-cut example for reasons that I shall give in chapter 2. Nevertheless I think the imperfection and contestability conceptions do exert a strong pull and play an important role as 'ideal types' to which particular accounts can be illuminatingly compared. I shall illustrate this point by examining four contemporary explanations of why moral and political disagreement is so intractable. I shall begin with C. L. Stevenson's account, move on to R. M. Hare's, and then finish with the more recent accounts of Alasdair MacIntyre and John Rawls.

---

[4] W. Connolly, *The Terms of Political Discourse*, second edition (Oxford: Martin Robertson, 1983), p. 226. In chapter 2, I shall raise doubts about whether a defender of an essential contestability thesis need accept a version of the contestability conception as I have characterized it.

[5] T. Ball, *Transforming Political Discourse* (Oxford: Blackwell, 1988), p. 13.

C. L. Stevenson

In *Ethics and Language*, Stevenson officially accords equal weight to two different considerations in explaining why moral and political disagreement occurs: he argues that characteristically it arises partly as a result of disagreement in (non-moral) *belief* and partly as a result of disagreement in *attitude*.[6] In this way he seems to combine elements from the imperfection and contestability conceptions: if (as it appears) he believes that disputes over the non-moral facts can in principle be resolved to the satisfaction of every reasonable person, then he accepts an element of the imperfection conception; he also accepts an element of the contestability conception because he allows that most moral and political disputes will be rationally irresolvable since they rest in part on differences in attitudes. But Stevenson does seem to give disagreement in attitude priority in explaining deep and persistent moral and political differences. Consider, for example, the following passage:

People with different racial or temperamental characteristics, or from different generations, or from widely separated communities, are likely to disagree more sharply on ethical matters than on factual ones. This is easily accounted for if ethics involves disagreement in attitude; for different temperaments, social needs, and group pressures would more directly and urgently lead these people to have opposed attitudes than it would lead them to have opposed factual beliefs.[7]

In this light Stevenson's account is best understood as an impure version of the contestability conception.

R. M. Hare

Hare argues that 'ought' in its moral sense has two logical properties. Anyone who uses it correctly is committed to *universalizing* her judgements and to recognizing their *prescriptivity*: firstly, if a person says that she morally ought to do something, she is logically commit-

---

[6] See C. Stevenson, *Ethics and Language* (New Haven, CT: Yale University Press, 1944), p. 11. In this respect Stevenson differs from another 'emotivist' who was writing at roughly the same time: A. J. Ayer. Ayer argues that in cases of moral disagreement the dispute is really about a question of fact, not about a question of value (A. J. Ayer, *Language, Truth and Logic*, second edition (New York: Dover, 1952), p. 110). In a new preface to the second edition, however, Ayer emphasizes that he did not mean to rule out the possibility of significant disagreement in attitudes (*ibid.*, p. 21).

[7] Stevenson, *Ethics and Language*, p. 18.

ted to the view that anyone in exactly the same circumstances as her ought to do the very same thing; secondly, she cannot sincerely assent to the claim that she ought to do something unless she does it when the circumstances arise in which she is able (psychologically and physically) to do so. In Hare's view, moral argument, properly conducted, involves exploiting these two logical features.

In *Freedom and Reason*, Hare leaves open the possibility, and indeed likelihood, of rationally irresolvable moral and political differences arising about what ought to be done when there are clashes between radically different ideals. For example, he considers the hard-core Nazi who is willing to universalize his claim that Jews ought to be exterminated and who accepts that if he were a Jew, he too ought to be killed.[8] In these cases rational argument comes to an end when all the facts have been agreed and the implications of the logical properties of moral discourse have been followed through. In this respect Hare's account incorporates an element of the contestability conception. However, he contends that the vast majority of actual moral and political disputes are not like the disagreement between the hard-core Nazi and the liberal. In his view most moral and political disagreement has one of three sources: a failure to agree on the (non-moral) facts; a failure of one or both parties to universalize their moral judgements fully; a failure of one or both parties to appreciate the prescriptivity of moral judgements.[9] So even though Hare's account in *Freedom and Reason* departs from the imperfection conception because it holds that some moral and political disputes occur despite no error of reasoning or failure of understanding, it does conform to that conception in other respects because it supposes that in practice disagreement mainly has its origins in thoughtlessness and insensitivity.

Since writing *Freedom and Reason*, however, Hare has changed his mind about the fanatic.[10] In *Moral Thinking* he argues that the logical properties of moral terms 'yield a system of moral reasoning whose conclusions are identical with that of a certain kind of utilitarianism'.[11] He maintains that *if* the fanatic's conclusions did coincide with the results of this form of utilitarianism, then they

---

[8] See Hare, *Freedom and Reason* (Oxford: Oxford University Press, 1963), ch. 9.
[9] See Hare, *Freedom and Reason*, especially ch. 6.
[10] See R. M. Hare, *Moral Thinking: Its Levels, Method and Point* (Oxford: Oxford University Press, 1981), ch. 10.
[11] Hare, *Moral Thinking*, p. 4.

would be correct, but he contends that in all real life cases the fanatic has simply reasoned badly. So Hare now seems to endorse a pure version of the imperfection conception of how persistent moral and political disagreement is to be explained because he is maintaining that when there is agreement on the (non-moral) facts, moral and political disagreement arises exclusively from errors of reasoning.

A. MacIntyre

In *After Virtue*, MacIntyre argued that contemporary moral and political disagreement is largely due to a clash between incommensurable ways of thinking about moral issues, some of which have been prised from the historical and social contexts that gave them their meaning. In MacIntyre's view, our current moral discourse consists of modern terms such as 'rights' and 'utility', which are moral fictions because they have no proper reference, co-existing alongside older concepts, such as the notion of desert, which have broken free from their original moorings. Different theories of justice, whether they are developed by political theorists or implicit in the arguments of 'ordinary non-philosophical citizens', contain elements which there is no rational way of comparing. Thus far at least MacIntyre seems to endorse a version of the contestability conception, for he seems to believe that key political concepts such as justice can reasonably be interpreted differently and be used to express incommensurable ways of thinking; the existence of political disagreement need not imply that someone has made a mistake.

In his more recent work, however, MacIntyre confronts a relativist challenge which maintains that on his account 'no issue between contending traditions is rationally decidable'.[12] MacIntyre responds to this challenge by arguing that disputes between different traditions of thought with their own norms of rational inquiry may nevertheless be rationally resolvable in some cases.[13] A particular tradition T1 may face an epistemological crisis in which it fails to deal with (what is for it) an important incoherence and in which

---

[12] A. MacIntyre, *Whose Justice? Which Rationality?* (London: Duckworth, 1988), p. 352.
[13] This does seem to mark a shift in MacIntyre's thinking even though he doesn't explicitly acknowledge it. For example, in *After Virtue: A Study in Moral Theory* (Notre Dame, IN: University of Notre Dame Press, 1981), he wrote: 'the facts of incommensurability *ensure* that protestors [against the invasion of someone's rights in the name of someone else's utility] can never win an *argument*' (*ibid.*, p. 69; first italics added).

another tradition T2 can provide a cogent and illuminating explanation *by the standards of T1* for why this incoherence has arisen.
MacIntyre argues that the Thomist tradition, which synthesizes
Aristotelianism and Augustinian Christianity, and which gives the
notion of desert a central place in its conception of justice, can be
vindicated in this way. He supposes that adherents to other traditions of thought and practice can be rationally persuaded to switch
allegiances, for each of these other traditions can be shown to have
failed in its own terms, and so by their own standards the Thomist
tradition provides a superior moral and political framework. In this
way MacIntyre is driven by the spectre of relativism to make space
for an idea which is part of the imperfection conception, viz. the idea
that a whole tradition of thought may be *mistaken*, even though he
believes that norms of rational inquiry are immanent in traditions
and cannot transcend them. In effect he attempts to combine
elements from each of the imperfection and contestability conceptions.

MacIntyre's account is not stable, however, for it tends to be
pulled back towards the contestability conception. It is unclear
that MacIntyre is justified in holding (as he seems to do) that the
correctness of some tradition – in his view, Thomism – can be
demonstrated from within each of the other traditions. In MacIntyre's view, unless a tradition overcomes an epistemological crisis it
is facing, it will be 'defeated' and adherents to it will be 'compelled' to change allegiances.[14] But surely it is natural to think
that there will almost always be scope for reasonable disagreement
over whether some tradition has solved a set of problems, and over
whether there are prospects for resolving these problems from the
standpoint of any other tradition when they are interpreted in its
terms. An epistemological crisis is unlikely to give *conclusive* reasons
to abandon a tradition. When reasonable disagreement does occur
over whether a tradition has been defeated, and over whether an
alternative tradition is better able to deal with the problems faced,
it is hard to see from the perspective of MacIntyre's theory how
one of these traditions might be true and the others false, for
MacIntyre denies content to the notion of truth independent of
tradition.

[14] See MacIntyre, *Whose Justice? Which Rationality?*, pp. 364–5.

J. Rawls ⸴

Rawls's recent writings have contrasted the disagreement that exists in modern constitutional democracies over particular conceptions of the good, which he thinks there is no reasonable prospect of eliminating without the use of coercion, with the disagreement over conceptions of justice that is also present in these societies, which he thinks there is some coherent hope of resolving rationally and non-coercively.[15] Rawls maintains that political philosophers in democratic regimes should accept that the existence of conflicting conceptions of the good is a permanent feature of the social landscape (that is, barring the oppressive use of state power), but should nevertheless strive to achieve consensus on which principles of justice ought to govern basic institutions. He argues that the concept of justice has a distinctive role to play in a constitutional democracy, viz. it can and should enable citizens to justify to each other their major institutions. In Rawls's view, this means that political philosophy in democratic regimes should have as its most important aim the achievement of 'an overlapping consensus', in which those who hold different comprehensive views of the good life converge on a single conception of justice. He claims that an overlapping consensus is valuable because in a democratic regime it will provide the basis for the public justification of principles of justice and the institutions which embody them. Public justification of this kind is valuable not only in itself but also because (and in so far as) it will make these societies enduring and stable. In order to facilitate it, Rawls thinks that political philosophy should employ 'the method of avoidance': whenever it is possible, controversial metaphysical claims and disputed conceptions of the good should not be invoked in advancing conceptions of justice.

The philosophical part of Rawls's project of achieving an overlapping consensus can be divided into two stages. First, the excavation of the shared stock of ideas that are implicit in the public culture; second, the presentation of these ideas in a novel form, thereby creating a new basis from which a rational consensus may be forged. Rawls claims that we need:

---

[15] See especially 'Justice as Fairness: Political Not Metaphysical', *Philosophy and Public Affairs*, vol. 14, 1985, pp. 223–51; 'The Idea of an Overlapping Consensus', *Oxford Journal of Legal Studies*, vol. 7, 1987, pp. 1–25; 'The Priority of Right and Ideas of the Good', *Philosophy and*

to discover and formulate the deeper bases of agreement which one hopes
are embedded in common sense, or ... originate and fashion starting points
for common understanding by expressing in a new form the convictions
found in the historical tradition.[16]

According to Rawls, the fundamental idea that is implicit in the
public culture of a constitutional democracy is the idea of 'political
society as a fair system of social cooperation between citizens
regarded as free and equal persons'.[17] The conception of justice that
Rawls advocates, which he refers to as 'justice as fairness', offers an
interpretation of this idea in a form that he hopes will be rationally
persuasive to inhabitants of democratic regimes.

If Rawls is correct, we are entitled to be relatively optimistic
about the prospect of agreement on a conception of justice, and
presumably also on conceptions of liberty and equality, since any
plausible conception of justice will need to be explicated by reference to interpretations of these concepts. Rawls argues that disputes
over which conception of distributive justice we should accept can
be resolved to the satisfaction of any reasonable citizen, so he in
effect rejects the contestability conception of how the fact of persistent political disagreement is to be explained, according to which
these disputes are in some sense part of the nature of the concept
itself. His rejection of the contestability conception is not straightforward, however, for he acknowledges that there are 'sources of
reasonable disagreement' in political life: for example, evidence
bearing on a question may be conflicting and complex, and hence
hard to assess and evaluate; there may be disagreement over the
amount of weight to attach to different considerations; our concepts
are vague and are subject to hard cases.[18] In Rawls's view, these
sources of reasonable disagreement will mean that even though we
can reach uncoerced agreement on a particular *conception* of justice,
we may continue to disagree on questions of how it is to be interpreted.[19]

Rawls seems sympathetic to the imperfection conception of why
disagreement over which conception of justice we should accept is so

Public Affairs, vol. 17, 1988, pp. 251–76; 'The Domain of the Political and Overlapping
Consensus', *New York University Law Review*, vol. 64, 1989, pp. 233–55.
[16] J. Rawls, 'Kantian Constructivism in Moral Theory', *Journal of Philosophy*, vol. 77, 1980,
p. 518.
[17] Rawls, 'The Idea of an Overlapping Consensus', p. 7.
[18] Rawls, 'The Domain of the Political and Overlapping Consensus', p. 237.
[19] *Ibid.*, p. 253.

intractable because he seems to be saying that if we are sufficiently ingenious, we will be able to design an argument that is rationally persuasive to all citizens of democratic regimes. He falls short of endorsing this conception of disagreement, however, because he is officially agnostic on the truth of moral cognitivism and this thesis is an essential ingredient of it. Rawls wishes to make possible the public justification of major institutions and in this way secure a morally acceptable basis for stability in the face of different views about how to live; if he were to assume the truth of moral cogniti-vism, and to claim that justice as fairness aims to be a correct theory of justice, he would thereby embrace a contentious metaethical thesis and make the achievement of an overlapping consensus correspondingly unlikely. He proposes instead 'to avoid the problem of truth and the controversy between realism and subjectivism about the status of moral and political values'.[20] However, there would be room for Rawls to endorse moral cognitivism purely as part of an account of how political disagreement is to be explained. He is not committed to neutrality over moral cognitivism except in so far as he is developing a conception of justice that can be the object of an overlapping consensus.

Rawls's position, like MacIntyre's, is unstable, however. His refusal to endorse moral cognitivism officially is difficult to sustain. It is unclear whether the public justification of major institutions, which an overlapping consensus makes possible, is valuable unless it employs a *correct* conception of justice. A shared conception of justice, supported by argument, might make the basic structure of a society mutually acceptable to its inhabitants, but it is not clear that in itself this is something to celebrate: suppose, for example, that an oppressed group were to agree on a conception of justice that had been worked up from ideas in the public culture of their society but which served to legitimate their subordination. False consciousness would make the major institutions of this society mutually accept-able but it is unclear that the kind of public justification it facilitated would be of any value. Surely public justification is valuable only if it employs a correct conception of justice. So it seems that Rawls does need to endorse a version of moral cognitivism if he is to explain when and why public justification is of value, even though he does not have to presuppose its truth in *arguing* for justice as fairness. Hence

---

[20] Rawls, 'Justice as Fairness: Political Not Metaphysical', p. 230.

he is only a short step away from an imperfection conception of why disagreement persists over which conception of justice we should accept.

I hope I have now said enough to show that the distinction between imperfection and contestability conceptions is a fruitful one and that it illuminates explanations of the persistence of political disagreement which do not fit neatly into one or the other.

2 THE ARGUMENT SKETCHED

The imperfection conception of how political disagreement is to be explained seems to gain some of its plausibility from the apparent weakness of the contestability conception and vice-versa. We tend to recoil from the imperfection conception to the contestability conception because it seems implausible to suppose that major political disputes could be resolved to the satisfaction of every reasonable person who has sufficient time, patience and sincerity, and who follows the laws of logic properly. On the other hand we tend to recoil from the contestability conception to the imperfection conception because we fear that it is committed to some unacceptable, perhaps even self-defeating, brand of moral relativism: witness MacIntyre.

Most theorists, who, like myself, are unhappy with the imperfection and contestability conceptions, try to avoid an oscillation between them by combining elements from each without endorsing either in its entirety. But the hard question is: which mix of elements provides the best explanation of why moral and political disagreement is so intractable? I propose to defend an account which, like the imperfection conception, makes room for the idea of moral truth and error but, like the contestability conception, denies that moral and political disputes are resolvable to the satisfaction of every reasonable person who has the time and interest to think through the issues involved and who is able to apply the laws of logic skilfully enough. This account includes a commitment to moral cognitivism, but gives a theory of error of the kind sought by the imperfection conception only a minor role. The imperfection conception supposes that if a moral and political belief is mistaken, its correctness can be demonstrated to the satisfaction of every reasonable person who is fully competent in applying the laws of logic and has the time at her disposal to do so. In consequence the theories of error developed from within it have included a demonstration (or an alleged demonstration) of the incorrectness of the views which are held to be mistaken. Since the account I propose does not make the assumption that mistakes can in general be demonstrated, it does not need to give a central role to a theory of logical error, i.e. a theory of why people make logical mistakes.

The structure of my argument is as follows. In the first chapter I shall discuss a pure version of the contestability conception of how the intractability of political disagreement is to be explained: the familiar idea that political disputes are value-laden and disputes over values, unlike disputes over facts, are not amenable to rational resolution. I argue against it that we do not have any general a priori reasons for thinking that disputes over facts are rationally settleable but disputes over values are not. It cannot be proved that those who disagree on moral and political issues start from different 'basic' value premises; this is at best a hypothesis. The most promising way of attempting to provide support for it is by making an epistemological contrast between ethics/politics and the natural sciences, in terms of the idea that the latter but not the former are governed by norms which, when properly adhered to, will produce convergence on an answer. This attempt fails, I argue, because there are also norms of inquiry in ethics and politics which make possible rational resolutions to disputes; in effect I defend a form of moral cognitivism, and thereby favour an element of the imperfection conception over this version of the contestability conception.

In chapter 2, I shall consider an apparent variant of the contestability conception which has received considerable attention in recent writings: viz. the thesis that key political concepts are essentially contested. I think this is the best candidate for an account of why political concepts are inherently disputable. But in its most defensible form, it does not constitute a genuine version of the contestability conception, for it does not deny that there may be uniquely correct interpretations of essentially contested concepts. Contrary to the view of some critics, it can be consistent to claim that a concept is essentially contested *and* that one interpretation of it is superior to others. The thesis of essential contestability need not deny the role of rationality in resolving disputes over the application of these concepts: it can maintain that even though disputes over essentially contested concepts are amenable to rational resolution,

they cannot be resolved by arguments of the sort that every reasonable person with sufficient logical skills must accept.

In the form in which I defend them, essential contestedness theses
are an attractive blend of elements from the contestability and
imperfection conceptions. Like the contestability conception they
suppose that disputes over key moral and political concepts cannot
be resolved to the satisfaction of every reasonable person who has
sufficient competence in applying the laws of logic and who thinks
through the issues but, like the imperfection conception, they
suppose that we can make sense of the idea of a mistake on moral
and political matters. Essential contestedness theses of this kind are
not wholly acceptable as they stand, however. I argue that they
need to be amended to give a proper role to contingent features of
moral and political discourse in explaining the extensiveness and
persistence of contemporary moral and political disagreement. I also
contend that the scope of essential contestedness theses may be more
limited than some imagine, for they may not play a part in
explaining the intractability of *all* persistent moral and political
disputes.

An apparent assumption behind the claim that concepts such as
'justice' are essentially contested appears to be that those who
interpret the *term* 'justice' differently nevertheless employ the same
underlying *concept*. That view has not gone unquestioned. Some try
to debunk the notion of an essentially contested concept by arguing
that many terms which are taken to express essentially contested
concepts are really ambiguous and hence disputes over them are not
genuine.[21] This idea gives rise to what I call 'the miscommunication
thesis', which I shall discuss in chapter 3: it holds that those who
occupy different moral and political standpoints simply talk past
each other and fail to engage. This thesis comes in two main
versions. The first endorses the imperfection conception of how
political disagreement arises and is to be explained, and is defended
notably by Locke, who maintains that people disagree because they
use the same terms to stand for different ideas, and use different
terms to stand for the same ideas. The second version endorses the
contestability conception and is a natural extension to morality and
politics of Thomas Kuhn's work in the philosophy of science; it
contends that those who advocate competing moral and political

---

[21] See, e.g. L. Allison, *Right Principles: A Conservative Philosophy of Politics* (Oxford: Blackwell,
1984), ch. 3, especially pp. 49–50, 54–5.

theories inhabit incommensurable conceptual frameworks. I argue against both of these versions and in doing so I implicitly defend the notion of an essentially contested concept against the objection that disputes over the proper use of key moral and political concepts are confused and not substantive.

Although, like the imperfection conception, the account I defend incorporates a form of moral cognitivism, it does not give a central role to a theory of error in explaining why moral and political disputes are so intractable. In chapter 4, I suggest that instead of seeking such a theory, we should construct purely empirical explanations that integrate rational considerations, i.e. the reasons people have (or think they have) for making the judgements they do, and 'non-rational' considerations, such as psychological propensities and social structures. A number of levels of explanation may be possible here, and particular explanations which are capable of operating at each of these levels are potentially very powerful. On the first level, a person's acceptance of a moral and political belief or theory might be accounted for in terms of a psychological propensity to be attracted to considerations which would provide some rational support for that belief or theory. On the second level, a person's psychological propensity to find these considerations attractive might itself be explained in terms of various experiences that she has had, or various influences to which she has been subjected. On the third level, some account might be given of why that person was likely to have been subject to that set of influences or experiences, and to have developed the relevant psychological propensity, in terms of her membership of some social group (e.g. class, race, sex).

I suggest that a specific variety of non-rational explanation, viz. *materialist* explanations, which appeal to the way in which power relations condition consciousness, have a crucial role to play. In chapter 5, the final chapter, I attempt to construct a particular materialist explanation for some political disagreement by employing a psychoanalytic theory developed by Nancy Chodorow on the differential effects of child-rearing practices (in the bourgeois family) on boys and girls and how these early experiences continue to affect later life. I claim that Carol Gilligan's research on gender differences in the approach to moral dilemmas and political issues can be explained by a Chodorowian theory. I apply the account I develop to account for the attraction of a conception of self-esteem that is to be found in the work of Robert Nozick.

CHAPTER I

Differences in values

One of the most common explanations for the extent and persistence of political disagreement exploits the idea that political differences, such as those which arise out of allegiances to competing conceptions of justice, rest upon differences in values. On this view, political disputes are intractable (largely if not entirely) because they involve disputes over values and disputes of this kind, unlike disputes over facts, are not rationally resolvable. It conforms to the contestability conception of how we should account for the intractability of political disagreement since it holds that moral and political thought is by its very nature open to dispute because of its value-ladenness.

Not all political disputes involve disputes over values. Some are concerned simply with the most efficient means to a shared goal. For example, people may disagree about the best means to reduce the level of unemployment in a society: they may agree that this is an important goal and about its significance in relation to other goals, but nevertheless disagree about the most efficient means to realize it. Many political disputes are value-laden, however. Some have to do with questions of justice, with what sort of institutions or arrangements a society morally *ought* to adopt. Others have to do with, for instance, how free or how democratic a society is, and reveal competing conceptions of freedom and democracy. Whether these kinds of disagreements are value-laden is a matter of some controversy. It has been argued that freedom and democracy are moral notions because they describe from the moral point of view;[1] if they are moral notions, then disputes over their proper interpretation may rest upon differences in values.

I shall consider some different but related premises that figure in

[1] See, e.g. W. Connolly, *The Terms of Political Discourse*.

16

versions of the hypothesis that the intractability of political disagreement is largely to be explained by its evaluative nature. Firstly, the general view that political positions start from incompatible and irreconcilable value assumptions. Second, the view that factual judgements aspire to describe the way the world is, whereas value judgements cannot be coherently understood as having such an aim. Third, the view that 'empirical' inquiry should follow a procedure which, properly applied, will lead investigators to converge on the same hypotheses, whereas ethical and political thought is not subject to any comparable method. In a single chapter I cannot give full answers to the profound questions in value theory which are raised by these issues but I hope to give some reasons for thinking that explanations of this kind are not promising.

I DO CONFLICTING POSITIONS REST ON DIFFERENT BASIC VALUE PREMISES?

The version of the explanation under consideration which is perhaps the most common holds that fundamentally opposed political positions rest upon incompatible 'basic' premises and these premises involve different value judgements. Let me define the expression 'basic premise': for my purposes, a premise is basic for a person if, and only if, she can have no further reasons for accepting it and no objections others bring to it count against it from her perspective, given her set of beliefs, the norms of rational argument she accepts, and those beliefs and norms she must accept on pain of unintelligibility. If disputants do have different basic premises, then it seems that they will not share enough ground for disputes between them to be settled by rational means.

Consider the abortion debate, which is sometimes used to illustrate this idea. Those opposed to abortion offer the following argument designed to show that the state should outlaw it:

(1) A foetus is an innocent human being;
(2) Intentionally killing an innocent human being is murder;
(3) Abortion involves the intentional killing of a foetus;
(4) Therefore, abortion is murder;
(5) Murder should be illegal.
(6) Therefore, abortion should be illegal.
   Those in favour of legally permitting abortions sometimes present the following counter argument:

(7) A person should be allowed to decide who (if anyone) can use his or her body;

(8) A foetus uses a woman's body;

(9) Therefore, a pregnant woman should be allowed to decide whether or not to permit the foetus to use her body.

(10) Therefore, abortion should be legal.

This may appear to be a paradigm example of two valid arguments both of which start from different basic value premises and which establish contradictory conclusions. But on reflection, it should be clear that neither (1), nor (7) nor (8) is a basic value premise in the sense described. (8) is not a *value* judgement according to any sensible criterion of what that involves; (1) and (7) are not basic premises, for those who accept them can in principle give reasons for doing so. Arguably (2) is a basic value premise, but only because it is a stipulative definition and, as such, can be accepted by an opponent for the sake of argument. (It is not unquestionably a basic premise since someone who accepts it may give as a reason for doing so the claim that if one understands properly the meaning of the expression 'intentional killing of an innocent human being' and the meaning of the term 'murder', one must accept the premise as true by definition.) (3) and (5) are perhaps basic premises but not ones that are disputed. (Arguably they are not even basic premises because further facts might be offered in support of each of them; it might be said that abortion involves the intentional killing of a foetus because a person who performs one cannot but intend to kill the foetus, and that murder should be illegal because it violates the rights of others.) Consequently the reconstructions provided do not show that the question of whether abortion should be legal or illegal relies on the acceptance or rejection of arguments that start from incompatible basic value premises.

In *After Virtue*, MacIntyre defends the idea under consideration, viz. that many moral and political disputes persist because those engaged in them have incompatible basic value premises.[2] For example, when he discusses the relation between Rawls's and Nozick's conception of justice, he concludes:

---

[2] The view presented in *After Virtue* is qualified in *Whose Justice? Which Rationality?*, chs 1 and 18. I discuss MacIntyre's account in my 'MacIntyre on Liberalism and its Critics: Tradition, Incommensurability and Disagreement' in J. Horton and S. Mendus (eds) *After MacIntyre* (Cambridge: Polity, forthcoming).

Rawls makes primary what is in effect a principle of equality with respect to needs ... Nozick makes primary what is a principle of equality with respect to entitlement ... For Rawls ... justice is made into a matter of present patterns of distribution to which the past is irrelevant. For Nozick only evidence about what has been legitimately acquired in the past is relevant.[3]

In MacIntyre's view, the theories Rawls and Nozick defend are more articulate and more coherent versions of political arguments presented by 'ordinary non-philosophical citizens'. They inherit the general problem that although the conclusions each arrives at can be logically derived from the premises from which they start, there is no shared rational way of deciding between them.[4]

What then are the different basic premises on which Rawls's and Nozick's theories rest? Consider the candidates which MacIntyre proposes.

For Nozick:[5]

(11) Each individual has inalienable rights;

(12) A distribution is just provided that everyone is entitled to what they have;

(13) A person is entitled to what he has provided that he acquired it by legitimate means.

For Rawls:[6]

(14) The principles of justice for any social order are those principles that would be chosen by a rational agent from behind 'a veil of ignorance' such that he does not know what his place in society will be.

Are any of (11), (12), (13) and (14) basic premises in the sense described? As MacIntyre points out, Nozick does not offer much in the way of argument for (11), apart from some vague remarks about the separateness of persons; however, others have tried to offer considerations in support of it and those who accept it certainly do not regard it as foundational. This implies that it is not a basic premise. Construed in a suitably broad way, (12) and (13) are perhaps basic premises but only because they can then be understood as analytic truths: the substantive issues would arise in relation to the question of how we determine people's entitlements and what

---

[3] MacIntyre, *After Virtue*, ch. 17.
[4] *Ibid.*, pp. 8, 231.
[5] *Ibid.*, pp. 230–1.
[6] *Ibid.*, pp. 229–31.

is to count as 'legitimate means'. (14) is not a basic premise; others have given reasons against it, and Rawls himself has defended it. So (11) and (14) do not seem to be basic premises, and even if (12) and (13) are basic premises, when they are understood in this way they turn out to be mutually acceptable.

It might be maintained that we merely have to go back further in order to demonstrate that both the abortion debate and the debate between Rawls and Nozick do hinge upon different basic value premises. This is not self-evidently true, however, and I do not know any way of reconstructing the various positions involved to show that it is the case. Logic alone does not require there to be basic premises. Our beliefs might fit together in such a way such that no one belief was unsupported by others. So the claim that there must be at least some basic premises in our moral and political thought is not a logical truth and the view that fundamentally different moral and political positions rest on incompatible basic premises is at best a hypothesis. Defenders of it must show how it is possible in principle for there to be different basic premises in value inquiry, and why we might expect there to be divergences of this sort.

2 WORLD-GUIDEDNESS AND CONVERGENCE

Some think that there can be, and often are, incompatible basic value premises in ethical and political thought because it is not 'world-guided' in an important sense. This supposedly explains why there is convergence on a body of beliefs in the natural sciences but not in ethics and politics. The general view that much ethical and political thought is not world-guided can be held independently of the idea that there are incompatible basic premises: for example, it can be held in conjunction with the view that there are incompatible but equally coherent systems of moral belief, none of which could be excluded on the grounds that they fail to represent the way the world is.

In its crudest form (which arguably cannot be combined with the idea that intractable disagreement arises because people are committed to different basic value *premises*), this sort of explanation holds that moral and political judgements are essentially expressions of emotion, and that when people disagree deeply in their moral and political judgements, they differ in *attitude*, not belief.[7] More sophis-

---

[7] See Russell, 'Science and Ethics'; cf. Stevenson, *Ethics and Language*, ch. 1.

ticated versions of it are also available. The germs of one are to be found in Gilbert Harman's work. For instance, he writes:

The observation of an event can provide observational evidence for or against a scientific theory in the sense that the truth of that observation can be relevant to a reasonable explanation of why that observation was made. A moral observation does not seem, in the same sense, to be observational evidence for or against any moral theory, since the truth or falsity of the moral observation seems to be completely irrelevant to any reasonable explanation for why that observation was made.[8]

Harman seems to be arguing that the best explanation for our moral 'observations' makes no reference to the existence of moral facts, whereas the best explanation for our 'empirical' observations may make reference to 'empirical' facts. So he apparently must rule out the possibility of an explanation of convergence in ethics which involves the idea that convergence has occurred *because* people have come to appreciate the moral facts, although he allows scope for an explanation of convergence in the natural sciences that appeals to the parallel idea that convergence has occurred because scientists have come to appreciate the empirical facts. It is a short step from here to the hypothesis that divergences in ethical and political thought can be explained in terms of the idea that this kind of thinking, unlike that in the natural sciences, is not guided by an independent reality.

A variant of this sort of explanatory contrast between ethics and politics and the natural sciences, with some important qualifications, can also be found in Bernard Williams's work.[9] He writes:

In a scientific inquiry there should ideally be convergence on an answer, where the best explanation of the convergence involves the idea that the answer represents how things are; in the area of the ethical, at least at a high level of generality, there is no such coherent hope.[10]

Williams does not explicitly claim that the contrast he makes between scientific and abstract ethical thought could be used to explain any ethical *disagreement*; however, he appears to think it could,[11] and this

---

[8] G. Harman, *The Nature of Morality: An Introduction to Ethics* (New York: Oxford University Press, 1977), p. 7.
[9] See B. Williams, *Ethics and the Limits of Philosophy* (London: Fontana, 1985), ch. 8.
[10] *Ibid.*, p. 136.
[11] *Ibid.*, p. 133.

would certainly be a natural application of the distinction he draws.[12]

There are at least two promising replies to the claim that the different degrees of convergence in ethics/politics and the natural sciences can be explained by the different extents to which these disciplines are world-guided: firstly, the argument that ethics and politics are just as world-guided as the natural sciences;[13] secondly, the argument that even if ethics and politics are not world-guided, there are nevertheless norms of inquiry, comparable to those in the natural sciences, which make possible rational convergence on a body of moral and political beliefs. Let me begin by considering the first reply.

In order to show that ethics and politics are just as world-guided as the natural sciences, content would need to be given to the notion of a moral *description*. Let us characterize moral realism as the view that there are moral facts which describe the world, and these facts are independent of the evidence for them. Some, such as David Brink, believe that ordinary moral practice – the form and content of our moral judgements, the way in which we approach our moral decisions, and our reactions to the behaviour of others – presupposes a commitment to moral realism:

Moral judgements are typically expressed in language employing the declarative mood; we engage in moral argument and deliberation; we regard people as capable both of making moral mistakes and of correcting their moral views; we often feel constrained by what we take to be moral requirements that are in some sense imposed from without and independent of us.[14]

Others have doubted whether ordinary moral discourse has any clear metaphysical presuppositions. This much seems true, however:

---

12 Williams would no doubt want to restrict the scope of an explanation of the extent and persistence of political disagreement which exploited his attempt to contrast ethics with the natural sciences. For example, he emphasizes that the contrast he is making is between natural scientific thought and *abstract* ethical thought, and distinguishes between concrete moral terms (such as 'bravery' and 'gratitude') and abstract ethical terms (such as 'right' and 'ought').

13 This would be ineffective against Harman's argument for he apparently claims that *even if* there were moral facts, they would be irrelevant to the explanation of why we make the moral judgements we do. But I think Harman is simply mistaken on this point and would concur with most of the arguments that Nicholas Sturgeon develops against it in his paper 'Moral Explanations', reprinted in G. Sayre-McCord (ed) *Essays on Moral Realism* (Ithaca, NY: Cornell University Press, 1989).

14 D. Brink, *Moral Realism and the Foundations of Ethics* (Cambridge: Cambridge University Press, 1989), p. 24.

if other spheres of discourse that have the same superficial appearance are to be understood realistically, then we need some grounds for refusing to understand moral and political discourse in the same way. Since the explanation for why moral and political disagreement is so intractable that I am considering treats scientific and other 'factual' claims as straightforward attempts to describe how things are, we need reasons for treating moral and political discourse differently. These reasons might seem to be provided by some apparent metaphysical and epistemological problems which arise out of the very idea of a moral reality.

J. L. Mackie marshalled what he called 'the argument from queerness' (which has both metaphysical and epistemological components) against any form of moral realism:

If there were objective values, then they would be entities of a very strange sort, utterly different from anything else in the universe. Correspondingly, if we were aware of them, it would have to be by some special faculty of moral perception or intuition, utterly different from our ordinary ways of knowing everything else.[15]

Mackie's metaphysical worry can be understood (at least in part) as an expression of the general concern that whatever entities, qualities or relations we admit into our ontology we should be able to give some philosophically respectable account of how they are connected to the world that natural science, and in particular physics, describes (since, according to the commonsense view at least, physics is the discipline which studies the ultimate constituents of reality). In the philosophy of mind, this concern has made it seem important that some form of materialism be true. Within ethical and political theory, the concern has exerted a different kind of pressure (one to which Mackie succumbed), viz. to deny that values are part of the fabric of the world and hence that there is anything evaluative that needs to be reconciled with the commitments of natural science. The moral realist, who accepts that value judgements can be descriptions of the world, needs a way of showing how it is that values can be genuinely part of the world despite the fact that natural science can (in some sense) give a complete account of reality. Moral realists have responded in a number of different ways to this part of the

---

[15] See J. L. Mackie, *Ethics: Inventing Right and Wrong* (Harmondsworth, Middlesex: Penguin, 1977), p. 38.

argument from queerness; I shall consider the strategy which has received the most attention.

Some moral realists have sought to answer the metaphysical part of the argument from queerness by drawing an analogy between values and secondary qualities such as colours, tastes and sounds. This may appear surprising since many philosophers have located secondary qualities in the mind rather than in the world; an analogy between values and secondary qualities would then tend to support a theory such as Mackie's which holds that we mistakenly project values onto the world. Moral realists such as John McDowell reject this way of viewing secondary qualities, however; instead of locating them in the mind, he and others conceive of them as properties in objects that cannot be adequately understood 'otherwise than in terms of dispositions to give rise to subjective states'.[16] An analogy between secondary qualities and moral values then provides a response to part of the argument from queerness: just as colours (and other secondary qualities) are part of the fabric of the world, even though a natural scientific account which described only those features of the world which are as they are independently of any perceiver would not mention them, so too, moral values are part of the fabric of the world even though such an account would not make any reference to them; just as colours are *supervenient* on physical properties but not reducible to them, so too values are supervenient on properties of persons, actions etc., but not reducible to them.[17]

The second part of Mackie's argument from queerness – the epistemological worry that moral realists are committed to the existence of 'some special faculty of moral perception or intuition, utterly different from our ordinary ways of knowing anything else' – can be countered by showing that use of the visual idiom in relation to ethical judgement doesn't require us to invoke some mysterious moral sense. Indeed, the analogy between visual perception and value experience can itself be made plausible by appealing to another use of the visual idiom – when talking about the detection of

---

[16] J. McDowell, 'Values and Secondary Qualities' in T. Honderich (ed) *Morality and Objectivity: A Tribute to J. L. Mackie* (London: Routledge and Kegan Paul, 1985), p. 113.

[17] The metaphysical part of the argument from queerness also includes a demand that we explain the action-guiding quality of moral judgements without appealing to the idea that moral values are 'intrinsically prescriptive entities' (Mackie, *Ethics*, p. 40). For different ways of dealing with this demand, see S. Lovibond, *Realism and Imagination in Ethics* (Oxford: Blackwell, 1983), section 13; J. McDowell, 'Are Moral Requirements Hypothetical Imperatives?', *Proceedings of the Aristotelian Society*, suppl. vol. 52, 1978, pp. 13–29; Brink, *Moral Realism*, chs. 3 and 4.

psychological phenomena – which can itself be understood in a metaphysically innocuous way. Sabina Lovibond, who defends a version of moral realism, draws attention to Wittgenstein's remarks on how we detect emotion in others. Wittgenstein says:

'We *see* emotion.' – As opposed to what? We do not see facial contortions and make inferences from them (like a doctor framing a diagnosis) to joy, grief, boredom. We describe a face immediately as sad, radiant, bored, even when we are unable to give any other description of the features ...[18]

Wittgenstein wants to insist that there is nothing philosophically distressing about the use of the visual idiom when talking of detecting emotions. Lovibond, correctly in my opinion, wants to make the same point in relation to the idea of 'seeing moral aspects of a situation'. Just as talk of seeing emotion does not commit us to some metaphysically weird faculty of psychological intuition, talk of seeing moral aspects of a situation or having moral perceptions, does not commit us to a metaphysically weird faculty of moral intuition. If we deem it appropriate to speak of a faculty of moral intuition, Lovibond suggests, we can think of it as amounting to nothing more 'than possession of the specific range of discursive skills which enable us to report on moral features of the world'.[19]

Although the idea of a moral reality is not as problematic as it might initially seem, there are still difficulties with it. The analogy I have described to make it plausible can only be pushed so far.[20] Moral realism stands in need of more refinement if it is to provide a satisfactory response to the proposal that there is convergence in the natural sciences but not in ethics and politics because the former, but not the latter, are world-guided – more refinement than it is appropriate for me to attempt in this context. Other apparent cases of supervenience, such as the relation between the biological and the chemical, or between the physical and the mental, might be better models for the relation between moral and non-moral facts. Even if

---

[18] L. Wittgenstein, *Zettel*, second edition, (ed) G. E. M. Anscombe and G. H. von Wright, (trans) G. E. M. Anscombe (Oxford: Blackwell, 1981). Quoted by Lovibond, *Realism and Imagination*, p. 47.

[19] Lovibond, *Realism and Imagination*, p. 50.

[20] For criticisms of the analogy between values and secondary qualities, see Williams, *Ethics*, ch. 8; S. Blackburn 'Error and the Phenomenology of Value' in T. Honderich (ed) *Morality and Objectivity* (London: Routledge and Kegan Paul, 1985); C. McGinn, *The Subjective View* (Oxford: Oxford University Press, 1983), ch. 8. Crispin Wright rejects standard objections to the analogy, but goes on to give his own argument for why it cannot provide support for moral realism: see C. Wright, 'Moral Values, Projection and Secondary Qualities', *Proceedings of the Aristotelian Society*, suppl. vol. 62, 1988, pp. 1–26.

we cannot provide a model of supervenience adequate for it, this does not show that moral realism is incoherent: it might merely show that moral properties are odd in the sense that nothing strictly comparable to them exists.[21] I shall not pursue these ideas further, however.

As I suggested earlier, there is another strategy that might be used in order to provide a justification for rejecting the proposal that disagreement in ethics and politics is explained (partly or wholly) by the fact that these disputes are not world-guided. We need to disentangle an epistemological and a metaphysical idea that often become entwined: first, the claim that convergence on a body of beliefs in the natural sciences might be explained by the idea that these beliefs correctly describe the way the world is; second, the claim that convergence in the natural sciences might be explained by the idea that investigators have conducted an inquiry using the same, proper methods. I propose that it is the second claim, not the first, which is intuitively appealing; and ethics and politics, no less than the natural sciences, might be held to be governed by a proper method even if the idea of a moral reality makes no sense.

In some disciplines (e.g. the natural sciences) the notion of 'proper method' is perhaps tied conceptually to the idea of an external reality: proper methods are *simply* those that enable us to discover facts about the way the world is.[22] But even if this is so, there is nothing incoherent in the idea that in other disciplines 'proper method' is merely what enables us to determine which views are rationally acceptable.[23] Someone who argued that there is such a thing as proper ethical inquiry, but who then denied that we could give any sense to the notion of an ethical reality, would need to give an account of what makes the method they advocate in ethics and politics the correct one if it is not that it enables investigators to

---

[21] See Brink, *Moral Realism*, p. 173.

[22] This idea would be rejected by some: see, e.g. J. Kenyon, 'Doubts About the Concept of Reason', *Proceedings of the Aristotelian Society*, suppl. vol. 59, 1985, especially p. 249; R. Rorty, *Objectivity, Relativism, and Truth. Philosophical Papers, vol. 1* (Cambridge: Cambridge University Press, 1991), especially pp. 34–45. Rorty thinks that what constitutes proper method is determined by the aims of a discipline, which in the case of the natural sciences are prediction and control; 'truth' is the term given to theories which realize these aims.

[23] Accounts such as those provided by R. M. Hare (see the introduction and ch. 1, section 4), Jürgen Habermas (see ch. 2, section 3) and Onora O'Neill (see *Acting on Principle: An Essay on Kantian Ethics* (New York: Columbia University Press, 1975); *Constructions of Reason: Explorations of Kant's Practical Philosophy* (Cambridge: Cambridge University Press, 1989)) are examples of this approach.

discover ethical facts which describe the world or get closer to them.[24]

Even if there is a conceptual connection in the natural sciences between 'proper method' and 'discovering the way the world is', the difference between explaining convergence there in terms of the idea that investigators have followed the proper method of inquiry and explaining it in terms of the idea that they have converged on the facts, can be brought out by noting how scientists might converge on a theory that misrepresents reality, despite following correct methods of inquiry. The best evidence available might support a theory which is in fact false: agreement on this theory might be explained by the idea that investigators had followed proper scientific practice but could not be explained by the idea that they had come to describe the world correctly. It is the idea that there is a correct scientific method (perhaps not codifiable, but a method nonetheless), employed by different scientists, which is more plausible as a candidate for explaining (partially, at least) actual convergence in the natural sciences. After all, how do we know that our currently accepted scientific theories are true? In the past, convergence has frequently occurred on scientific theories which have turned out to be false. What reasons do we have for thinking that the theories we accept today are true descriptions of the world? They may have greater explanatory power than those they have replaced, and may be *closer* to the truth, but this isn't sufficient to show that they *are* true. Just as convergence in the past is not explicable in terms of coming to describe correctly the way the world is, it is far from clear that convergence on present scientific theories can be explained by the idea that these theories correctly represent how things are. If we explain convergence in the natural sciences by saying that investigators have followed proper method, we might then unpack the notion of 'proper method' in terms of the idea that it is constituted simply by those procedures which enable us to get closer to the truth, but that would not make our explanation of convergence reducible to the thought that convergence has occurred because reality has been correctly represented.

---

[24] One possibility would be a Wittgensteinian account which held that what counts as a reason or a proper method of inquiry is determined by moral practice: see S. Hurley, *Natural Reasons: Persons and Polity* (Oxford: Oxford University Press, 1989) especially chs. 1–2. Other possible accounts are provided by R. M. Hare (see ch. 1, section 4) and Onora O'Neill.

It might be argued that in discussing these issues we should be concerned only with *ideal* cases of convergence, i.e. cases in which convergence occurs on a set of beliefs that do describe the way things are. Williams, who (as I noted earlier) contrasts the world-guidedness of the natural sciences with the predicament of abstract ethical thought, might appear to hold this position because he argues that the distinction he is making 'does not turn on any difference in whether convergence will actually occur and it is important that this is not what the argument is about'.[25] But if it is claimed that actual convergence in the natural sciences is non-ideal, then the alleged contrast between ethical thought and the natural sciences cannot explain actual convergence or divergence in these disciplines. Later it becomes clear that Williams would not be happy with entirely divorcing the ideal from the actual since it is the existence of actual convergence which he thinks makes plausible the view that convergence in ideal cases can be explained in terms of world-guidedness:

it would be unrealistic to disconnect these ideas totally from the way in which the history of Western science since the seventeenth century is to be understood. The conception of scientific progress in terms of convergence cannot be divorced from the history of Western science because it is the history of Western science that has done most to encourage it.[26]

Williams's position seems to be that convergence in the natural sciences is to be explained (generally, but not always) in terms of the idea that investigators have conducted an inquiry using the same, proper methods. He can of course add that what *makes* some method in the natural sciences correct is the fact that when it is employed, it generally leads us (closer) to the truth. But if Williams wants to contrast the natural sciences and ethics/politics in the way I have suggested, he needs to justify the claim that ethics/politics, in contrast with the natural sciences, are not governed by a set of norms which permit rational convergence on a body of beliefs and which would account for any convergence that comes about. He apparently needs to show that uncoerced agreement in the natural sciences can be secured because well-conducted inquiry makes possible rational resolutions to disputes in them, whereas there are no

[25] Williams, *Ethics*, p. 136.
[26] *Ibid.*, pp. 136–7.

comparable norms of inquiry which make possible rational resolutions to disputes in ethics/politics.

Some defenders of moral realism are inclined to argue that there are no *deep* disanalogies between scientific method and method in ethics.[27] Hypotheses in the natural sciences may be confirmed or falsified by observations, but these observations are theory laden in such a way that it may be rational occasionally to reject some background theory presupposed by an observation (and hence the observation itself) rather than to reject a hypothesis that conflicts with it. Similarly it might be argued that in ethics we should construct theories about what is right or wrong, just or unjust, and compare these to the particular moral judgements we make. Particular judgements would then play the same role in ethics that observations play in science: they would not be immune to revision, and indeed would be revised if they conflicted with a normative theory that systematized enough of our most fundamental considered judgements, but would nevertheless be a significant test of our moral theories.[28] Even if particular judgements did not possess the same reliability in ethics that observations do in the natural sciences, they could play a role in ethical inquiry that was otherwise analogous.[29]

The idea that ethical inquiry and scientific inquiry are deeply analogous deserves serious consideration. But it does tend to credit abstract ethical theory with a role which it lacks in much ordinary ethical thought. We might conclude that ordinary ethical thought is defective because it is insufficiently theoretical but this should surely only be a consequence of paying careful attention to it. (Moral realists such as Brink are committed to taking ordinary practice seriously given the importance they attach to the idea that moral realism is presupposed in it.) In the next section I propose to pay some attention to the actual practice of moral and political argument: my aim is not merely to describe it but rather to show how it can be reconstructed in a way that makes it plausible to regard it as an exercise of rationality rather than as, say, mere rhetoric or propaganda. To be justified in rejecting the idea that disagreement

---

[27] See, e.g. Brink, *Moral Realism*; R. Boyd, 'How to Be a Moral Realist' in Sayre-McCord (ed) *Essays on Moral Realism*.
[28] See J. Rawls, *A Theory of Justice* (Oxford: Oxford University Press, 1971), pp. 20–2, 48–50. Rawls's view is discussed further in section 4 of this chapter.
[29] Cf. Brink, *Moral Realism*, p. 138.

in ethics and politics is widespread compared to disagreement in the natural sciences because the latter as opposed to the former is governed by a method which, properly applied, will lead to convergence, all we need to do is show that ethics and politics, properly conducted, are governed by rational processes which, in principle at least, could lead to convergence. We do not need to show that moral and political inquiry and scientific inquiry are analogous in any deeper sense. My ultimate goal is to vindicate a coherentist theory of justification in which particular moral and political judgements are accorded respect even though they are not regarded as incorrigible, and the construction of theory is regarded as less important in ethics and politics than it is in the natural sciences.

3 ORDINARY MORAL PRACTICE

Moral and political debate is dominated by the use of analogical arguments: particular cases are described in order to support a conclusion and persuade opponents to accept that conclusion. Consider disagreements over whether the bombing of Libya in 1986 was an act of state terrorism. During disagreements such as these, analogical arguments are often employed. Paradigm cases are invoked which many would be prepared to agree are acts of terrorism and it is argued by analogy from them.[30] We ask ourselves in what ways the case under consideration is like the paradigm cases and whether the differences are relevant or not. For instance, some might compare the bombing of Libya with the IRA pub bombings in Britain during the 1970s. They might argue that these are relevantly similar on the grounds that just as the IRA sought to create a climate of fear in mainland Britain in order to secure their political aims, so too the US sought to create a climate of fear among states who they believed were supporting terrorism, in order to force them to end that support. Others will favour the United States's own account of its actions, viz. that the bombing of Libya was an act of self-defence based upon intelligence information they had received which indicated that Libya was going to sponsor terrorism against their interests abroad, and therefore conclude that there is no

---

[30] To forestall possible misunderstanding, I should point out that by talking of paradigm cases I do not mean to imply that these are incontestable examples of terrorism. My use of 'paradigm' is similar to Ronald Dworkin's: see *Law's Empire* (London: Fontana, 1986), pp. 72–3.

analogy with the IRA pub bombings. Further differences of interpretation will no doubt emerge: some will argue that the civilian deaths which resulted from the Libyan bombing constituted murder because they were inevitable and predictable, just like the deaths of the civilians in the pub bombings; others will argue that there is a deep disanalogy between the cases on the grounds that the IRA targeted civilians whilst the US merely targeted sites from which they believed terrorism was being orchestrated, and hence will conclude that in the latter case the deaths of the civilians was a side-effect rather than an intended outcome.

Constructing analogies enables us to reflect upon what considerations make an act of violence terrorist and in this way by moving to a higher level of abstraction we can rationally resolve disagreements about what constitutes terrorism. When we are unsure about whether some act constitutes terrorism, we may construct analogical arguments merely by describing cases where we have more reason to be confident of our judgement (even though further reflection may throw that into doubt). This involves making judgements about what features of these cases are relevant, and to that extent involves abstracting from their particularity, but it does not require the construction of general principles. Similarly when we raise questions about whether some act of terrorism is right or wrong – or whether terrorism is necessarily or always wrong – we can do so by describing other cases, e.g. cases where innocent people are killed but not as a result of terrorism, or cases in which terrorism secures good ends. None of this need involve us in the construction of general principles.[31]

Consider a related set of disputes over the concept of violence itself.[32] Some Marxists see negligence over safeguards in the workplace or the implementation of policies that lead to unemployment as central examples of acts of violence. Liberals typically deny that these are correctly described as acts of violence: their paradigms are

---

[31] But can't at least *prima facie* general principles be constructed simply from a judgement about what is morally relevant in the cases under consideration? The thought here would be that if some feature is morally relevant in one situation, it will be so in others and therefore its presence will provide a *prima facie* reason for drawing some moral conclusion. However, it may be the case that which features of a situation are morally relevant sometimes or always depends on what other features are present: see J. Dancy, 'Ethical Particularism and Morally Relevant Properties', *Mind*, vol. 92, 1983, pp. 530–47.

[32] See J. Harris, 'The Marxist Concept of Violence', *Philosophy and Public Affairs*, vol. 3, 1974, pp. 192–220, for an interesting discussion of what is at issue among those who have different conceptions of violence.

cases of murder, rape and armed robbery in which those who perform acts of violence are, in principle at least, easily identifiable and commit them intentionally. Liberals accuse these Marxists of not having the conceptual tools to discriminate between, e.g. earthquakes that cause harm and suffering and failures to implement safety measures in the workplace, thereby being logically compelled to count both as acts of violence. They respond by pointing out that safety measures in the workplace are, at least, under some group of people's control who could have implemented them, whereas earthquakes could not be prevented by human intervention. Liberals reply that there is a morally basic difference between acts and omissions: if part of the point of the concept of violence is to assign responsibility, then it should not be applied to failures to implement safety measures since no one is responsible for omissions of this kind. The Marxists describe omissions for which agents are morally culpable (e.g. failing to rescue a child who is drowning in a shallow pool) and try to show the similarity between these cases and cases, for example, when safety measures fail to be implemented. Rational resolution to particular disagreements may be achieved at any stage in these arguments, but even if it is not, there is always the possibility that rationally persuasive analogies will be found.

The standard view is that analogical reasoning should be construed as inductive. Copi, for example, claims that all analogical arguments can be cast in the following general form, where a, b, c and d are any entities and P, Q and R are any attributes:

a, b, c, d all have attributes P and Q
a, b, c all have the attribute R
Therefore, d probably has the attribute R[33]

But it is unclear whether the arguments I have in mind could be correctly represented in this way. With moral and political analogical arguments, we can list similarities between the controversial case, and the case with which it is being compared (i.e. the analogue). To the extent that the analogy is successful, we might say that the listed similarities support the conclusion that is drawn, but the notion of probability has no clear application unless it is being used as a synonym for 'better supported', for it is obscure how, even

[33] I. Copi, *Introduction to Logic*, sixth edition (London: Collier-MacMillan, 1982).

in principle, numerical values could be assigned to the degree of support provided by the premises.

It seems plausible to divide analogical arguments into different varieties. These varieties have a common underlying structure:

Case A has the features a, b, c,..., n
Case B has the features a, b, c,..., n
....
Case X has the features a, b, c,..., n−1
Therefore,
Case X has the feature n as well

Although analogical arguments have this common structure, they may involve one of a number of different sorts of inference. In some cases the inference is warranted by a causal connection between features a, b, c,..., n−1 and n; these are the sort of analogical arguments on which Copi focuses. In other cases the inference is justified by a 'logical' or conceptual relation between features a, b, c,..., n−1 and n. *If* moral and political analogical arguments fall into either of these categories, they must surely fall into the second one. So, it might be argued, in good arguments of this kind the relation between the features a, b, c,..., n−1, and n should be deductive, and therefore these arguments must be deductively formulable. But if a moral or political analogical argument was successfully represented in deductive form, from a purely logical point of view the analogue would be unnecessary. Let me explain this claim by looking at an analogy that is sometimes appealed to within the debate over the moral acceptability of abortion.[34]

Imagine a case in which a person (A) wakes up to find that someone (B) has been connected to his (A's) kidneys because B's own no longer function properly. Only A can keep him alive because they share a rare blood group, and no machine could play the same role. Many people's reflective judgement is that A has the right to disconnect B despite the fact that he will die if he is disconnected from A. Now consider a case in which a woman wants an abortion. She consented to intercourse (but not, one might add, to pregnancy) and is in good physical health so would suffer only the standard (but still significant) risks and disabling effects of child bearing. By analogy, we conclude that even if we concede that the

[34] The analogy is essentially the same as the one presented by J. J. Thompson in 'A Defence of Abortion', *Philosophy and Public Affairs*, vol. 1, 1971, pp. 47–66.

foetus is a person, the woman has the right to abort the foetus. More formally, we might represent the argument in the following way:

Analogue:
(1) B is a person.
(2) A did not consent to B's use of his body.
(3) B will die if he is disconnected.
(4) B cannot survive if he is not connected to A.
(5) But A has the right to disconnect B.

Controversial case:
(1') The foetus is a person.
(2') The woman did not consent to the foetus's use of her body.
(3') The foetus will die if the woman has an abortion.
(4') The foetus cannot survive if it is not connected to the woman.
Therefore, by analogy,
(5') But the woman has the right to abort the foetus.

Now *suppose* this analogy is deductively valid. What this amounts to saying is that (5) follows deductively from (1) – (4) and (1') – (4') have the same logical form as (1) – (4). But if (1') – (4') have the same logical form as (1) – (4), then (5') must follow deductively from (1') – (4') in just the same way that (5) follows deductively from (1) – (4). (1) – (5) are irrelevant to the question of whether (1') – (5') is a deductively valid argument; furthermore, (1) – (5) are unnecessary from a logical point of view and can add only persuasive force to the argument (1') – (5').

We might conclude from this that good moral and political analogical arguments must be susceptible to formulation deductively and therefore the analogue is, logically speaking, unnecessary: if a full description of a disputed case yields a moral or political conclusion deductively, then there is no need to find or construct an analogue to that case in order to justify the conclusion. Another position is possible, however: these arguments need not be construed as (approximations to) deductive arguments and evaluated in these terms, but rather can be assessed *simply* according to whether there are any relevant dissimilarities between the cases presented. This involves abstracting from the particular cases but need not involve constructing deductive arguments. Although analogical arguments are assessable in terms of similarity between the analogue and the controversial case, there may be good moral and political analogical arguments which cannot, in practice at least, be formulated deductively. Formulating an analogical argument deductively involves listing all the elements in the analogue that support the moral or political judgement made from it, then showing that the controversial case is structurally similar to the analogue. But, in practice at least, it may not be possible to list all the relevant elements in the analogue: the potential complexity of situations which are confronted militates against the construction of the general principles and exceptions clauses that are needed in order to formulate deductively moral or political arguments concerning what ought to be done and what is just or unjust.[35]

My reconstruction of ordinary moral reasoning has given a central place to analogical arguments which are concerned with particular judgements and do not require the formulation of general principles in order to justify them. But are analogical arguments which are not deductively formulable genuine arguments, or are they merely pieces of rhetoric that on occasions can have great persuasive force? Many of those who are inclined to deny the genuineness of these arguments are unwilling to countenance the existence of forms of ethical reasoning other than the deductive;[36] They insist that all good moral arguments must be open to formulation in deductive terms. This position often seems to be motivated by a prejudice, however; John McDowell identifies this prejudice and offers an interpretation of Wittgenstein's remarks on rule-following in order to dispel it. McDowell takes Wittgenstein's target in these remarks to be the idea that 'acting in the light of a specific conception of rationality must be expressed in terms of being guided by a universal principle'.[37] If, say, one's applications of a moral or political term were capturable by a universal formula – which, on

---

[35] This view was Aristotle's: see, e.g. *The Nicomachean Ethics*, (trans) W. D. Ross (Oxford: Oxford University Press, 1980), v, 10. See also J. McDowell: 'to an unprejudiced eye it should seem quite implausible that any reasonably adult moral outlook admits of codification ... If one attempted to reduce one's conception of what virtue requires to a set of rules, then, however subtle and thoughtful one was in drawing up the code, cases would inevitably turn up in which a mechanical application of the rules would strike one as wrong – not necessarily because one had changed one's mind; rather one's mind was not susceptible to capture in any universal formula' ('Virtue and Reason', *The Monist*, vol. 62, 1979, p. 336).
[36] In *Reasoning and the Explanation of Actions* (Brighton: Harvester, 1980), ch. 5, David Milligan offers a critique of the idea that deduction provides the standard for a good argument.
[37] McDowell, 'Virtue and Reason', p. 337.

the view under consideration, they must be if they are to be genuine exercises of rationality – then any argument presented using that term which wasn't mere rhetoric could, in principle, be coaxed into deductive form.

In the relevant passages of the *Philosophical Investigations*, Wittgenstein considers a series of concept applications – exercises of rationality – that can be formulated in terms of a rule of this kind.[38] He asks us to imagine a pupil who is taught to continue the series 0,2,4,6 by adding two. The pupil continues the series up to 1000 and then beyond 1000 he writes down 1004, 1008, 1012, ... An immediate reaction to this example is to think that the misunderstanding can be cleared up by specifying more precisely what it is that the teacher wants the pupil to do; that is, the teacher's intentions – what the teacher means – determine one series that uniquely satisfies the description 'carrying on in the same way' and it is merely a matter of giving an accurate enough account of these intentions. On this view, the pupil wrote down the correct continuation of the series he thought the teacher meant him to write down, but this is not the series the teacher intended and if the teacher gave a more exact description of his or her intentions, this would resolve the unclarity in the instructions.

But, as Wittgenstein points out, misunderstanding could persist:

We say to him: 'Look what you've done!' – He doesn't understand. We say: 'You were meant to add *two*: look how you began the series!' – He answers: 'Yes, isn't it right? I thought that was how I was *meant* to do it.'[39]

Any instruction can be variously interpreted in just the same way that any sequence of numbers can be interpreted so as to satisfy a variety of different algebraic formulae. We can imagine a pupil who had received the instruction 'add two' reaching 1000 and writing down 1004, 1008, 1012 etc., then insisting that he had done what he was asked. As Wittgenstein suggests, we might conclude that he had understood the instruction 'add two' in the way that we would understand 'add 2 if the resultant sum is less than or equal to 1000, but add 4 if the resultant sum is greater than 1000'. Any further attempts to clarify the teacher's directions can be met by similarly unconventional construals. Just as a sequence of numbers always

---

[38] See L. Wittgenstein, *Philosophical Investigations*, third edition, (trans) G. E. M. Anscombe (Oxford: Blackwell, 1967) (hereafter referred to as PI), sections 185ff.
[39] PI, section 185.

underdetermines how that sequence is to be carried on, the correct past applications of any term do not determine one set of future projections that uniquely count as carrying on in the same way. Nor is there a unique interpretation of any set of rules or principles for the term's correct use which could provide us with such a set of future projections, for each formulation of a rule is itself susceptible to different interpretations.

I share McDowell's view that the purpose of Wittgenstein's discussion is not to raise sceptical doubts concerning whether any of us can ever be correctly said to be going on in the same way,[40] but rather to free us from a compelling assumption about what needs to be the case if it is to be true that we are – viz. that we must be interpreting some rule or principle and that this interpretation can be formulated. Wittgenstein's suggestion, on this reading, can be expressed in the following way: acceptance of the idea that if someone is genuinely carrying on in the same way (i.e. genuinely exercising rationality), then there must be some formulable rule governing their applications of a term, is motivated by the assumption that only if such a rule could be formulated could there be an act of grasping a rule which would uniquely determine what it is to carry on in the same way and thereby give a standpoint from which to assess the rationality of all the particular applications of that term. Wittgenstein's point against this assumption is that even when there is a formulable rule for the application of a term, that rule can be described or formulated in a number of different ways, each interpretation producing a different determination of what it is to carry on in the same way. So the postulation of the necessity for formulable rules to underwrite genuine exercises of rationality cannot do what it was hoped it would, viz. yield a standpoint independent of particular applications from which to assess the rationality of a practice.

The prejudice that if someone is genuinely applying a term consistently, or carrying on in the same way, then the applications of that term must be formulable into a set of rules or principles, is revealed in a conviction about the form rational resolutions of

---

[40] So I agree with McDowell that Saul Kripke's presentation of Wittgenstein's argument as it struck him (Kripke) is not an accurate representation of Wittgenstein's argument. See S. Kripke, *Wittgenstein on Rules and Private Language* (Cambridge, MA: Harvard University Press, 1982); J. McDowell, 'Wittgenstein on Following a Rule', *Synthese*, vol. 58, 1984, pp. 325–63.

disputes over 'hard cases' in ethics must take if they are possible at all. McDowell describes this conviction as the belief that:

the inconclusiveness of one's arguments stems merely from an inability, in principle remediable, to articulate what one knows. It is possible, in principle, to spell out a universal formula which specifies the conditions under which the concept, in that use of it which one has mastered, is correctly applied. That would elevate one's argument to deductiveness.[41]

Elevating one's argument to deductiveness would, of course, distinguish it from mere rhetoric. But Wittgenstein's claim (on McDowell's interpretation) is that genuine exercises of rationality do not need to be formulable deductively; so there may be arguments that are not mere rhetoric which nevertheless do not fit the deductive mould.[42]

Even if it were true that unless we could at least in principle (though perhaps not in practice) formulate any good moral or political argument deductively, then nothing could distinguish those that weren't formulable in this way from mere rhetoric, it is unclear how such a view could inspire us with confidence that the many moral and political arguments we intuitively regard as good are any different from mere rhetoric. No transcendental justification can be given for the conviction that arguments that are not in practice formulable deductively could in principle be coaxed into deductive form, so it remains a faith. If we want to resist those non-cognitivists who in effect view moral arguments as mere rhetoric (and if we want to provide an account of how convergence might, in principle, be reached on a body of ethical beliefs through rational procedures) rather than ask ourselves what has to be the case in order to satisfy a view of moral reasoning as at least implicitly deductive, we would do better to look (albeit with a critical eye) at our actual practice of

---

[41] McDowell, 'Virtue and Reason', p. 340.
[42] Perhaps the most direct attack on the idea that consistent application of a term – the condition rationality imposes on language use – requires that there be some formulable rule for the use of that term, is to argue that there are 'cluster concepts' (see Connolly, *The Terms of Political Discourse*, second edition, p. 14), or 'family resemblance terms'. Wittgenstein's suggestion that we 'look and see', rather than start with the presumption that there must be some set of properties that mark off, for example, all the activities we quite justifiably call games, has some force (see PI, section 66). But if we simply look, it may be the case that we are attending at the wrong level of generality – if we look for similarities between board games, card games, ball games etc. in terms of whether they all involve competition between players or winning and losing, or whether they involve skill or luck, we may be looking for common properties at the wrong level of generality.

moral and political argument. This is what I have tried to do in this section.

Argument by analogy, which is commonly used in moral and political debate, is a powerful method that does not require that we give universal formulae for the correct application of terms and thereby elevate arguments to deductiveness. When these arguments are rationally efficacious, they persuade people to extend the application of a term to cases they had previously thought dissimilar by showing that they are relevantly similar. This involves abstracting from the particular cases to some extent but does not necessarily involve constructing a deductive argument. The provision of universal formulae – whether in the guise of general principles or in the form of definitions that supposedly give necessary and/or sufficient conditions for the correct application of a term – may be insufficient in cases in which disagreement is simply transferred to the question of what the correct universal formula really is. This is often what happens if someone argues that we should apply a term to some case which fails to satisfy a proposed definition. This fact shouldn't make us doubt the possibility of resolving moral and political disputes rationally, however, since the provision of universal formulae is unnecessary for this purpose in cases in which people can be rationally persuaded without them. Indeed, it is often possible to reach rational agreement over the application of moral and political terms to particular cases despite the fact that no such agreement can be secured on universal formulae for the correct employment of them.[43] (This is not to deny that *sometimes* the formulation of general moral and political principles about what ought to be done, or general analyses of concepts, can be effective in resolving disputes.)

4 MORAL INTUITIONS AND A COHERENTIST THEORY OF JUSTIFICATION

I have defended the view that moral and political thought is governed by norms of inquiry which allow the possibility of arguing from particular cases in order to resolve disagreements rationally without appealing to general principles. These analogical argu-

---

[43] If Wittgenstein is correct in thinking that there are family resemblance terms, and some political terms are of this kind, then disagreement over general analyses of them may simply result from the fact that the use of the term in question cannot be captured by any general formula.

ments are not inductive in character, so they differ from many of those in the natural sciences. The idea that there are legitimate forms of moral reasoning which start from points of moral agreement would be challenged, however, by those such as R. M. Hare who think that 'moral intuitions' never provide a reason for drawing moral conclusions. Hare's rejection of the use of moral intuitions in moral argument rests on the thought that they may simply be a result of prejudice or stupidity, and that different people will often have different intuitions which will then generate different conclusions.[44] Surely this thought is correct. But recognizing that it is correct does not warrant the strong conclusion which Hare wants to draw, that the *only* legitimate method for rationally resolving moral disputes is by appeal to the logical property of universalizability.[45]

I am doubtful whether universalizability, as Hare understands it, is simply a requirement imposed by the meaning of the moral terms we employ, and hence dubious whether it provides a route via which substantive moral conclusions can be established independently of our moral intuitions.[46] But I shall not pursue this issue here: if Hare is correct, then the general thesis I am defending – that there are norms governing ethical thought which make possible rational resolutions to moral and political disputes – will receive further support. Instead, I will argue that even if it were possible to avoid the use of moral intuitions in moral argument, rational resolutions to moral disagreements could still be secured whilst using at least some of them.[47] I will do so by sketching a coherentist theory of moral justification and offering some defence of it.

[44] See Hare, *Moral Thinking*, p. 12.

[45] See especially Hare, *Moral Thinking*, 1 1.3; 'The Argument from Received Opinion' in R. M. Hare, *Essays on Philosophical Method* (London: Macmillan, 1971). Hare makes a distinction between moral and linguistic intuitions. In his view, it is a *linguistic* intuition, shared by fully competent speakers, that judgements involving moral notions such as 'ought', 'right' and 'wrong' are universalizable; it is a *moral* intuition that, e.g. slavery is wrong, when this judgement is not a result of universalization. Hare would allow that intuitions have a legitimate role to play in the resolution of disputes over the proper use of terms such as 'freedom' and 'democracy' for he would hold that these intuitions can be linguistic, and need not be moral. Keith Graham, however, would claim that even these disputes should not be resolved by an appeal to intuitions, irrespective of whether the intuitions are of the sort that Hare would characterize as linguistic: see his 'Regulative Political Theory: Language, Norms and Ideology', *Political Studies*, vol. 33, 1985, pp. 19–37. I shall not consider Graham's arguments but I think the kind of response I give to Hare's arguments can also be given to them.

[46] See Mackie, *Ethics*, ch. 4.

[47] My purpose in arguing against Hare is to defend the idea that there is a *diversity* of forms that rational resolutions to moral disputes might take. A single method, such as Hare's,

According to a coherentist theory of justification, the holding of a belief p (moral or otherwise) is justified if, and only if, p is part of a coherent system of beliefs and p's coherence at least partially explains why one holds p.[48] Defenders of coherentist theories of justification need to give some account of the relation of coherence. To say that a belief p coheres with other beliefs is to say more than that it is merely *consistent* with these other beliefs, for we surely want to allow that p coheres with them only if it does not *undermine* them. If p undermines some beliefs, then it does not cohere with them, even if they form a mutually consistent set. I suggest that the most plausible coherentist theory of justification will not go further than this, however: in particular it will not hold that a belief coheres with others *only if* it entails, or is entailed by, them; nor will it hold that a belief coheres with others only if it best explains, or is best explained by, them. It should allow the possibility of independent (or relatively independent) clusters of belief that are nevertheless justified; they cohere because they are mutually consistent and do not undermine each other.

Why should we accept a coherentist theory of justification? Brink argues that foundationalist theories of justification are incoherent on the grounds that there can be no beliefs that are non-inferentially justified or self-justifying in the way that foundationalism requires. He claims that if justifying beliefs must themselves be justified (or, at least, justifiable) any justified belief must be supported by appeal to *other beliefs*.[49] It is not clear that Brink has successfully refuted foundationalist theories, however, for one might plausibly ask why the requirement that justifying beliefs themselves be justified requires them to be justified by other beliefs rather than, say, by the fact that certain conditions obtain. I might be justified in believing that I am seeing a chair because I am perceiving the relevant object under conditions favourable for perception even if I had no second order *beliefs* about what kind of conditions were favourable for perception. That is to say, one might defend an externalist theory of *justification*, just as some have defended an externalist theory of *knowledge*. An externalist theory of knowledge holds that a person may know that p even though he is unaware of satisfying one or all of

---

would provide grounds for thinking that these resolutions are possible *if* it yielded determinate conclusions. I am not sure that it does.

[48] See Brink, *Moral Realism*, p. 103.

[49] *Ibid.*, ch. 5, section 5.

the conditions which make it true that he knows that p: for example, Alvin Goldman supposes that A knows that p, if and only if (i) p is true, (ii) A believes that p, (iii) p is justified, (iv) the fact that p causes A's belief that p;[50] and the fact that p causes A's belief that p may be something of which A is unaware. Similarly one might defend an externalist theory of justification according to which A may be justified in believing that p by satisfying some condition that he or she was unaware of satisfying:[51] for example, I might be justified in believing that Bill Clinton is President of the United States if my belief is acquired through reliable procedures, and my belief might be justified in this way although I do not have any beliefs about what kind of methods are reliable for establishing its truth. Even if Brink's arguments against foundationalist theories of justification are insufficient to refute them, however, the version of a coherentist theory of moral justification I have sketched is plausible because of the difficulty of finding foundational beliefs, i.e. beliefs in ethics and politics that are self-evident, self-justifying or non-inferentially justified. If a coherentist theory is correct, a first order ethical 'intuition' will be justified provided that it coheres with other beliefs (whether moral or non-moral); so too with ethical principles, normative ethical theories and metaethical beliefs. Of course (as Hare would no doubt point out) it may be the case that there are incompatible but coherent sets of moral beliefs, and these would be equally justified according to a coherentist theory of justification. But in this respect the predicament of moral and political thought is no different from that of inquiry in the natural sciences: there could also in principle be incompatible but coherent sets of beliefs about the natural world which stand up to the available evidence. We have no more reason to think that inquiry in ethical and political thought is so radically underdetermined that it excludes the possibility of rational resolutions to any or most moral and political disagreements than we have to think that scientific inquiry is radically underdetermined in this way.

In *A Theory of Justice*, Rawls describes the method of reflective equilibrium, part of which might be thought to be required by a coherentist theory of justification. The method of reflective equi-

---

[50] See A. Goldman, 'A Causal Theory of Knowing', *Journal of Philosophy*, vol. 64, 1967, pp. 355–72. See also R. Nozick, *Philosophical Explanations* (Oxford: Oxford University Press, 1981), ch. 3 for a defence of an alternative externalist theory.

[51] See J. Dancy, *Introduction to Contemporary Epistemology* (Oxford: Blackwell, 1986), 9.2–9.4.

librium requires us to separate out a class of especially reliable judgements (or at least judgements that are not especially unreliable) from our ordinary moral judgements. However, the process by which considered judgements are identified is contentious and, I shall argue, should not be incorporated into a coherentist theory. According to Rawls, considered judgements are identified by sifting through our intuitions and separating out those 'in which our moral capacities are most likely to be displayed without distortion'.[52] Rawls believes that the kind of conditions under which our moral judgements are likely to suffer distortion are no different from the conditions under which *any* judgement is likely to fail to track the truth: we should discard judgements 'made with hesitation, or in which we have little confidence' and 'those given when we are upset or frightened or when we stand to gain one way or the other'.[53] It is not at all obvious that the kind of judgements which Rawls is seeking to exclude are especially unreliable, however.[54] Hesitation or lack of confidence may have many psychological explanations and is not a particular sign of liability to error; and it is not clear that strong emotions are any more likely to distort thinking than they are to focus it and thereby produce insight. Our interests are so frequently at stake in the moral judgements we make that few of our intuitions would survive if all those in which we stand to gain or lose significantly were excluded. So Rawls's procedure for identifying considered judgements threatens to exclude too much. I suggest that which of our moral beliefs are likely to be erroneous will be established by producing arguments against them, not by trying to determine non-moral criteria for when our general capacity for judgement is likely to be impaired which may then be applied to moral judgements in particular. No particular first-level moral belief will be immune to revision – any of them may in principle be mistaken – but, *pace* Hare, critical thinking is entitled to include them as premises, provided they pass the test of coherence.

A coherentist theory of moral justification might maintain that we should seek general moral and political principles about what ought to be done, and general criteria of rightness or justice. But coherentist theories of moral justification are also compatible with a particularism that denies the possibility of finding true, general moral

---

[52] Rawls, *A Theory of Justice*, p. 47.
[53] *Ibid.*
[54] I owe the thoughts that follow to a talk given by James Griffin.

principles about what ought to be done, or true general analyses of concepts such as rightness or justice. Particularists can hold that justification merely requires coherence between different contextual judgements, and that if a person makes a different judgement about two situations, she should be able to pick out a relevant difference between them; genuine inconsistencies between different particular judgements are to be resolved by abstracting from particular cases to this extent, and by rejecting the judgement which coheres less well with the others, not by constructing general principles. It is also possible to hold a hybrid view that some true but limited general moral and political theories are available which are justified by their coherence with our contextual judgements. For my purposes, I do not need to commit myself to any one of these accounts; I merely need to have shown that a coherentist theory of justification, with its commitment to consistency and to the idea that beliefs should not undermine each other and ideally should support each other, and a respect for particular moral judgements, provides a plausible account of the norms which govern moral and political thought. Moral and political thought may give less importance to the construction of general theory than does inquiry in the natural sciences, but it is nevertheless governed by norms that make possible rational resolutions to disagreements, and which at least sometimes make them possible without recourse to the construction of theory.

Susan Hurley defends a coherence theory of what it means to say that something ought to be done, i.e. a coherence theory of moral truth; on her account, to say that something ought to be done is to say that it is the act favoured by the theory (whichever it may be) that gives the best theory of the relation between the general moral concepts (such as right and ought) and specific moral concepts (such as just or kind).[55] Although a coherence theory of moral truth requires a coherence theory of moral justification, the latter does not require the former. Moral realists, such as Brink, may worry that a coherence theory of truth rules out a genuine possibility: that there could be equally coherent sets of moral beliefs, one of which correctly represents the way the moral world is but not the other. Aside from this doubt (which may ultimately be misplaced), the particular version of a coherence theory of moral truth defended by

[55] See Hurley, *Natural Reasons*, especially pp. 10–12, 264.

Hurley perhaps gives too great a role to theory in the determination of what ought to be done. On her account, to say that something ought to be done is to be committed to the existence of *some* theory that does the best job of displaying coherence; deliberation about what ought to be done when conflicting ends are at stake involves attempting to discover this theory or some part of it, and requires the formulation of principles. Hurley discusses a particular case of conflict between considerations of three sorts, viz. entitlement, equality and excellence.[56] She suggests that deliberation in this case involves a number of stages after these considerations have been identified: the deliberator must develop *conceptions* of entitlement, equality and excellence; then she must specify the relationship within each conception of the *principles* which constitute it, and also the relative weights of entitlement, equality and excellence in the specific situation under consideration. The upshot of my discussion of the role of the particular in moral deliberation is that there may not be any theory of this kind, viz. one which specifies values and principles in the way Hurley describes, which could in practice be formulated, whether partially or completely.

The claim that political disputes are intractable because political differences rest upon differences in values, and disputes over values are not rationally resolvable, has been found problematic. The general thesis that different moral and political positions rest on different basic value premises cannot be demonstrated and is at best a hypothesis. Attempts to underwrite it by the idea that ethics/ politics, unlike the natural sciences, are not world-guided were found to be unsatisfactory. Moral and political thought is governed by a set of rational procedures which make possible uncoerced convergence on moral and political conclusions. But it might be argued that the considerations I have so far presented leave room for a plausible position which I have not yet discussed: even if there are norms regulating moral and political thought, these norms allow great scope for reasonable disagreement and therefore we should expect divergences in belief. (Perhaps they underdetermine moral inquiry but not so radically that rational resolutions to all or most moral and political disagreements are ruled out.) That view might seem also to conform to the contestability conception of why it is that political disagreement is so pervasive and persistent, because it

---

[56] *Ibid.*, pp. 219–22.

appeals to the idea that moral and political thought is inherently open to reasonable dispute. In the next chapter, I shall consider it in the context of a discussion of the notion of an essentially contested concept.

CHAPTER 2

The notion of an essentially contested concept

The thesis that key political concepts are essentially contested appears to be a self-conscious version of the contestability conception of how political disagreement is to be explained:[1] W.B. Gallie introduced the notion of an essentially contested concept by saying that they are concepts whose nature it is to be open to endless dispute.[2] Many have regarded the notion as a fruitful one,[3] and some of them have thought that it provides an explanation for the intractability of disputes over the correct application of central social and political terms amongst professional theorists and others. I shall defend the thesis that key political concepts are essentially contested against some influential criticisms and shall argue that it contains insights about the nature of political disagreement. In its most defensible form, however, it does not constitute a genuine version of the contestability conception because in that form it does not deny that there may be uniquely correct interpretations of essentially contested concepts. Understood in the way I propose, essential contestedness theses combine elements from the imperfection and contestability conceptions: they hold that there is room for reasonable disagreement over the proper interpretation of key political concepts but argue that one particular interpretation may

---

[1] This chapter is a revised version of an article which appeared under the title 'On Explaining Political Disagreement: the Notion of an Essentially Contested Concept', *Inquiry*, vol. 33, 1990, pp. 81–98.

[2] W. B. Gallie, 'Essentially Contested Concepts', *Proceedings of the Aristotelian Society*, vol. 56, 1955–56 (hereafter referred to as ECC), p. 169; *Philosophy and the Historical Understanding* (hereafter referred to as PHU) (London: Chatto and Windus, 1964), p. 158.

[3] See, e.g. Connolly, *The Terms of Political Discourse*; Hurley, *Natural Reasons*, ch. 3; S. Lukes, 'Relativism: Cognitive and Moral', *Proceedings of the Aristotelian Society*, suppl., vol. 48, 1974, pp. 165–89, *Power: a Radical View* (London: Macmillan, 1974); A. MacIntyre, 'The Essential Contestability of Some Social Concepts', *Ethics*, vol. 84, 1973, pp. 1–9; D. Miller, 'Constraints on Freedom', *Ethics*, vol. 94, 1983, pp. 66–86, 'Reply to Oppenheim', *Ethics*, vol. 95, 1985, pp. 310–14.

nevertheless be correct and the others mistaken. However, I shall contend that even in this form they stand in need of qualification, for some contingent features of contemporary moral and political discourse make possible disagreement over key political concepts and help to explain why it occurs.

I ESSENTIALLY CONTESTED CONCEPTS

According to Gallie, an essentially contested concept is appraisive: it accredits a valued achievement. This accredited achievement is complex, i.e. made up of a number of different elements; explanations of why the achievement is valuable make reference to these elements, which disputants weight differently. Those who give particular weights to the elements acknowledge that others weight them differently. Furthermore, the accredited achievement admits of unpredictable modification in the light of changing circumstances.[4]

As examples of essentially contested concepts, Gallie gives the concepts of democracy, social justice, work of art and a Christian life. Consider his justification for classifying the concept of democracy as essentially contested. It accredits a valued achievement. This achievement is internally complex (Gallie claims) because it makes reference to three elements: the *power* of the people to choose and remove governments; *equality of opportunity* to attain positions of political leadership and responsibility; *active participation* of citizens in political life at all levels.[5] These elements which contribute to the valued achievement are weighted differently by contestants. Furthermore, the concept of democracy is open in character because 'democratic targets will be raised or lowered as circumstances alter'.[6]

Gallie might also have added, in the way that more recent writers such as William Connolly have done, that the concept of democracy is contestable not only because people can (without contradiction or absurdity) attach different weights to these elements but also because they may interpret them differently:[7] what counts as having the power to choose and remove governments, what counts as

---

[4] Gallie added three further conditions which were designed to distinguish essentially contested concepts from ambiguous terms, disputes over which may be simply confused. These will be considered in the next chapter.
[5] ECC, p. 186; PHU, p. 179.
[6] ECC, p. 186; PHU, p. 180.
[7] Connolly, *The Terms of Political Discourse*, p. 11.

equality of opportunity to attain political positions and what constitutes active participation in political life, are all matters of dispute.
So one essentially contested concept is related to a group of other
concepts whose proper uses are themselves contested, perhaps also
essentially.

Not all defenders of essential contestability theses employ this
model. Steven Lukes, for example, claims that the concept of power
is essentially contested[8] but does not characterize it in terms of different elements that disputants weight differently. According to Lukes,
all can agree that A exercises power over B if A affects B in a manner
contrary to B's interests.[9] Contestants disagree over the proper use of
the expression 'exercising power over' despite sharing an abstract
definition because they interpret the term 'interests' differently.

According to essential contestability theses, there is a non-trivial
sense in which disputes over the application of political terms such as
'democracy', 'freedom' and 'social justice' are *political* disputes. If
these concepts are essentially contestable, then it is mistaken to
suppose that we could have value-free accounts of the correct way of
using them and reserve the value judgements for the question of what
forms of social and political organization are desirable. Rather, a
person's use of terms such as 'democracy', 'freedom' and 'social
justice' in itself provides an account of what she thinks constitutes, or
would constitute, a desirable social order. Generally speaking, the
use of each of these terms is related to, and in some cases presupposes,
a range of uses of other key political expressions in such a way that
together they constitute an ideology.

Essential contestability theorists go one stage further than value
pluralists such as Isaiah Berlin and Bernard Williams. Williams
endorses Berlin's view that:

there is a plurality of values which can conflict one with another, and which
are not reducible to one another; consequently, that we cannot conceive of
a situation in which it is true both that all value-conflict had been elimi-
nated, and that there had been no loss of value on the way.[10]

Although Williams thinks that conflicts of values are most vivid
when they are experienced by a single consciousness, it is clear he
believes that many moral and political disputes *between* people also

[8] Lukes, *Power*, p. 9.
[9] *Ibid.*, p. 27.
[10] B. A. O. Williams, 'Conflicts of Value', *Moral Luck: Philosophical Papers 1973–1980* (Cambridge: Cambridge University Press, 1981), p. 71.

have their source in the way in which value conflicts admit of
different resolutions that are reasonable: 'sane and honourable
people can attach different importance to different values, so they
will not agree on the resolution of many conflict cases'.[11] But if
essential contestability theses are correct, people will also disagree
over how to *describe* values such as freedom, social justice and
democracy properly (and therefore over what counts as freedom,
social justice and democracy) because they can reasonably disagree
over how much weight to attach to the elements that contribute to
the achievement accredited by these concepts, or (on Lukes's
account) over how to interpret abstract definitions of them. Gallie's
account in effect proposes that we should model disputes over
essentially contested concepts on conflicts between values, for disputes over an essentially contested concept occur when people
attach different weights to the elements which contribute to the
achievement designated by it. Just as we aim to resolve conflicts
between values by asking which balance is the best, so we aim to
determine what (say) democracy is by asking which weighting of the
different elements that make up the concept is the best.

2 CAN ONE CONCEPTION OF AN ESSENTIALLY CONTESTED CONCEPT BE JUSTIFIABLY REGARDED AS SUPERIOR TO OTHERS?

Gallie seems to believe that disputes over essentially contested concepts are rationally unresolvable. If essential contestability theses
are committed to this view, they appear to be either relativist or
sceptical. Either they affirm the view that if a concept is essentially
contested, it admits of a variety of different conceptions, none of
which is better than the others from an objective standpoint, in
which case they seem to be relativist; or they affirm the view that if a
concept is essentially contested, it admits of a variety of conceptions,
and that none of these conceptions can be justifiably regarded as
better than the others from an objective standpoint, in which case
they seem to express a form of scepticism. On both views, there is an
apparent inconsistency in claiming that some concept is (a) essentially contested *and* (b) has an interpretation that can be justifiably
regarded as superior to others. It would be difficult to give up the

---

[11] *Ibid.*, p. 80.

idea that one interpretation of an essentially contested concept can be justifiably regarded as superior to others without rendering *philosophical* disputes over these concepts pointless. Perhaps some propagandist or other purpose might be served by engaging in disputes over the proper interpretation of essentially contested concepts. But it is unclear how we could come to a better understanding of what democracy is, or what social justice is, by engaging in disputes over the proper use of these terms if there were no possibility of establishing that particular interpretations can be justifiably regarded as superior to others.

In any case, defenders of essential contestability theses such as William Connolly and Steven Lukes apparently believe that sometimes at least we are warranted in regarding one conception of an essentially contested concept as better than others. In his book *The Terms of Political Discourse*, Connolly advocates particular interpretations of concepts such as 'power', 'freedom' and 'interests' by giving reasons in favour of them. He seems to deny (b),[12] but his remarks leave it unclear how he proposes to reconcile his rejection of (b) with the presentation of arguments in favour of particular interpretations of key political concepts in the body of the book. Furthermore, despite denying (b) he claims that 'a strong case can sometimes be made … in support of a particular reading'.[13] How this could be consistent with a rejection of (b) is obscure. In *Power: A Radical View*, Lukes argues that the concept of power is essentially contested and that the radical conception is superior to the liberal or reformist conception. As Brian Barry points out in a review of Lukes's book, if the concept of power is essentially contested, then it follows that no conception of power can be straightforwardly superior to another. So Lukes is inconsistent in claiming that the radical conception is better than both the 'liberal' and the 'reformist' conceptions, unless he simply means that from the radical standpoint this conception is the best of the three – and he certainly seems to be claiming something more substantial.[14]

Christine Swanton has tried to defend Lukes by arguing that essential contestability theses need only maintain that if a concept is essentially contested, either it admits of a number of different interpretations none of which is the *best*, or it admits of a variety of

---

[12] See Connolly, *The Terms of Political Discourse*, p. 226.
[13] *Ibid.*, pp. 226–7.
[14] See B. Barry, 'The Obscurities of Power', in *Government and Opposition*, vol. 10, 1975, p. 252.

different interpretations none of which can be justifiably *regarded as the best*.[15] Swanton proposes that although essential contestedness theses hold that 'there is no best conception [of an essentially contested concept], or none knowable to be best, some conceptions may nevertheless be better than others'.[16] On this view, even if a particular conception of an essentially contested concept can be shown to be the best of a known range of alternatives, there is always the possibility that some new conception will be developed that is superior to this one. Therefore, according to Swanton, Lukes can consistently claim that the concept of power is essentially contested and that the radical conception is better than its rivals, but not that the radical conception is the *best* conception of power. It is unclear, however, that this proposal will extricate Lukes from the difficulty that Barry and others have raised with his claims. Lukes maintains that each conception of power he distinguishes has its origin in a particular moral perspective[17] and holds that:

moral judgements may be incompatible but equally rational, because criteria of rationality and justification in morals are themselves relative to conflicting and irreconcilable perspectives.[18]

If the three views of power Lukes distinguishes are expressive of different moral perspectives, and criteria of rationality and justification are relative to a perspective, then there is no objective or even shared standpoint from which one of these views is, or can be justifiably regarded as, superior to the others. So Swanton's solution to the problem is not available to Lukes.

If it can be demonstrated that one conception of power is superior to a range of others in the way that Swanton wants to allow, it would seem that the concept of power cannot be essentially contested *with respect to* all of these different conceptions. This goes against Lukes's apparent belief that the concept of power is essentially contested with respect to the 'liberal', 'reformist' and 'radical' conceptions he distinguishes. Nevertheless I think it can be consistently claimed that the concept of power is essentially contested with respect to these different conceptions and that one of them is justifiably regarded as superior to the others – but only on a different view of

[15] See C. Swanton, 'On the "Essential Contestedness" of Political Concepts', *Ethics*, vol. 95, 1985, pp. 815–16.

[16] *Ibid.*, p. 815.

[17] See Lukes, 'Relativism: Cognitive and Moral', pp. 186–7.

[18] *Ibid.*, p. 178.

what is entailed by classifying a concept as essentially contested. The position I have in mind claims that if a concept is essentially contested, then it admits of a variety of different interpretations more than one of which are reasonable. If a range of different interpretations of a concept is reasonable, this does not imply that none of them is the best; nor does it imply that none of them can be justifiably regarded as the best. But it does follow that when the strongest reasons favour one conception of an essentially contested concept, and hence that it can be justifiably regarded as the best, people who refuse to accept this conception in the face of these reasons (on the grounds that they are unpersuaded by them) need not be unreasonable even though they are mistaken.[19]

Lukes would have to make major revisions to his theoretical framework before he could accept this view of what follows from classifying a concept as essentially contested. As I pointed out earlier, he implicitly denies that the strongest reasons could favour one particular conception of an essentially contested concept from an objective standpoint because he argues that competing conceptions of an essentially contested concept are embedded in different conceptual schemes and involve incompatible but 'equally rational' moral judgements. Lukes has perhaps revised his theoretical framework significantly in recent writings. His work now focuses on the idea that some values, goods and options are incommensurable, rather than on the idea that some moral standpoints employ incommensurable 'conceptual schemes'.[20] The idea that some values are incommensurable can be used in the way I have been indicating to model disputes over the proper application of an essentially contested concept. Lukes's considered view, however, seems to be that when values are genuinely incommensurable and conflict, then there is no correct way of balancing the different claims they make. In that case, if the application of an essentially contested concept involves balancing conflicting value components which are incommensurable, Lukes is committed to the view that there can be no correct way of doing so; therefore the problem of how one application of an essentially contested concept can be justifiably regarded as better than its rivals remains unresolved.

---

[19] So they need not be obliged to abandon their views 'on pain of forefeiting . . . self-respect and the regard of the scholarly community' (Barry, 'The Obscurities of Power', p. 252).

[20] See S. Lukes, *Moral Conflict and Politics* (Oxford: Oxford University Press, 1991), especially ch. 3.

The understanding of an essentially contested concept I propose could be accepted by William Connolly without his theoretical framework suffering too much damage. He holds the problematic position that when he argues for a particular interpretation of an essentially contested concept, he is not thereby claiming that this interpretation is superior (see above). But he also offers us another formulation of his position which he apparently thinks is equivalent: when he argues for a particular reading of an essentially contested concept, he is not claiming that it is '*demonstrably* superior to every other it opposes'.[21] These are not two different statements of the same position. But if Connolly were to make the second claim only, he could allow that particular conceptions of essentially contested concepts may be justifiably regarded as superior.

Understood in the way I suggest, the core of an essential contestability thesis is in its rejection of the view that if an argument is a good one, it ought to persuade any reasonable person who accepts its premises and who can apply the laws of logic properly. But how can it be reasonable to affirm the premises yet deny the conclusion of a good argument? Deductive arguments have the character that anyone who accepts the premises must, on pain of absurdity, accept the conclusion. So it could never be reasonable to accept the premises yet deny the conclusion of a deductively valid argument. What about inductive arguments of the sort that are involved in the choice between competing scientific theories? In these arguments, by definition the conclusion does not follow deductively from the premises.[22] Nevertheless it would still seem that it is unreasonable to affirm the premises yet deny the conclusion of a good inductive argument: if a particular scientific theory is better confirmed than another then it is unreasonable for a person to continue to subscribe to the less well-confirmed theory. However, one important contribution that Thomas Kuhn's work has made to the philosophy of science is the idea that there is no neutral algorithm for theory choice which, properly applied, will lead all scientists to converge on the same scientific theories. To accept this idea is not necessarily to move towards a non-rationalist model of scientific method of the sort that Kuhn appeared to advocate at various points in *The Structure of Scientific Revolutions*: a scientific rationalist can allow that there is

---

[21] Connolly, *The Terms of Political Discourse*, p. 226, emphasis added.

[22] Here I am assuming that an argument is inductively strong if it is improbable that the conclusion is false if the premises are true but the argument is *not* deductively valid.

room for what W. H. Newton-Smith describes as *judgement* in the practice of science, for:

[r]easonable men may be expected to have reasonable disagreements about what to do in the circumstances. There is no knock-down proof of superiority at the time that the choice has to be made.[23]

Sometimes it clearly will be unreasonable for a person to persevere with a scientific theory in the face of good arguments against it. But in other central cases of theory choice, it will not be unreasonable to do so: here there is scope for the idea that a person may make a reasonable judgement but not the judgement that is on balance the best.

This idea can be exploited to show that it is possible to believe consistently that a concept is essentially contested, and that one interpretation of it can be justifiably regarded as superior to the others. A defender of an essential contestability thesis can consistently deny the relativist version described earlier because she can argue that one conception of an essentially contested concept may be better than others, but allow that someone who mistakenly does not endorse it need not be unreasonable and need not have misapplied the laws of logic. She can also consistently reject the sceptical version. This version does not follow from the idea Gallie expresses that 'it is quite impossible to find a *general principle* for deciding which of two contestant users of an essentially contested concept "uses it best"'.[24] Even if there is no such general principle available, one can have reasons for favouring a particular conception of an essentially contested concept over another. A belief that some conception is better than its rivals may be warranted by the reasons in favour of it even though others reasonably deny that it is the best available. When they do so, they reason incorrectly, but their failure is best regarded as a lack of judgement (in Newton-Smith's sense), not as an incorrect application of the laws of logic (whether deductive or inductive) to the particular case. Gallie comes close to endorsing the position I have been describing when he writes: 'there can be little question but that greater or lesser degrees of rationality can be properly and naturally attributed to one continued use, or one

---

[23] W. H. Newton-Smith, *The Rationality of Science* (London: Routledge and Kegan Paul, 1981), p. 234.

[24] ECC, p. 189; PHU, p. 184 (Gallie's emphasis). Swanton seems to think that a sceptical thesis does follow from this claim of Gallie's (see Swanton, 'On the "Essential Contestedness" of Political Concepts', p. 814) but it's not clear to me why she thinks so.

change of use, than to others'.[25] The idea that disputes over the application of essentially contested concepts are not resolvable by arguments which have the character that they should persuade any reasonable person who accepts their premises and applies the laws of logic correctly, and hence that different uses of these concepts are reasonable, is what I take to be central to essential contestability theses.[26] Arguably it is entailed by the relativist version and by the sceptical version, although it does not by itself entail either of them.

The idea that there is a form of reasoning or 'judgement' in ethics and politics which establishes a conclusion, even though a person may reasonably refuse to endorse that conclusion despite agreeing on the considerations which count in its favour, is not unproblematic. The view that a person may reasonably refuse to give up a scientific theory even though the best reasons support a competitor is controversial. Since it is contentious it does not provide a clear paradigm to which defenders of essential contestability theses can appeal. A commitment to the (admittedly weaker) idea that an argument may establish a conclusion but permit reasonable disagreement, however, does seem to be incurred by anyone who holds two other views about morality and politics: firstly, the view that there is an irreducible plurality of values which conflict and, secondly, that it is not always an arbitrary matter, from the point of view of practical rationality, how we resolve clashes between values. If we hold these two views, we need to make sense of the idea that (sometimes at least) we can exercise our judgement in order rationally to balance out the different considerations that compete against each other when values conflict, and if we adopt that view it is a short step to allowing that a person who balances out these considerations differently may be mistaken, but need not be unreasonable.

Joseph Raz stipulates that two values are *incommensurable* if neither is better than the other and they are not of equal value.[27] If two values are incommensurable in this sense, then conflicts between them are not rationally resolvable. Just as conflicts between values may be rationally unresolvable because it is impossible to say that one trade off produces greater value compared to another, so too

[25] ECC, p. 191; PHU, p. 186.

[26] This idea is central to Gallie's account: see ECC, pp. 188–9, PHU, pp. 183–4; ECC, p. 196. It is also central to Connolly's: in his view, 'no single use [of an essentially contested concept] can be advanced that must be accepted by all reasonable persons' (Connolly, *The Terms of Political Discourse*, p. 40).

[27] J. Raz, *The Morality of Freedom* (Oxford: Oxford University Press, 1986), p. 322.

there may be no way in which we can rationally resolve disputes over (for instance) whether some institution is democratic, because it is impossible to say that giving more weight to one of the elements which contributes to the achievement which would thereby be accredited produces more value than any alternative weighting. But it is unclear that we are ever entitled to be confident that two values, or two value components, are incommensurable in this way. Raz discusses the concept of a good novelist, which Gallie and others might well regard as essentially contested: 'a good novelist might be judged by his humour, his insight, his imaginativeness and his ability to plot. It is possible that our weighting of the different criteria does not establish a complete ranking of all possible combinations'.[28] Raz seems correct to suppose that a dispute over whether one novelist was better than another *may* be rationally unresolvable because there may be no means of weighting these elements against each other in order to arrive at a uniquely correct judgement about their relative merits. But even though this kind of incommensurability is a genuine possibility, it is unclear that we could be warranted in claiming that it is present, for neither inspection nor engagement in a dispute over the proper weighting of the elements will justify the belief that they are incommensurable. We cannot distinguish the presence of incommensurability from a situation in which better judgement, or a more accurate perception of how the competing considerations should be weighted, is possible and warrants a definite conclusion; furthermore, where a more accurate perception is possible, there may be no independent criterion which can be used to show that this perception *is* more accurate than the others. Philosophical arguments concerning how the different elements should be weighted retain their point because we cannot say that there is no uniquely correct way of balancing one element against the others. Such a weighting might be possible even if anyone's claim to have provided it could be reasonably disputed.

3 WHY ARE DISPUTES OVER ESSENTIALLY CONTESTED CONCEPTS INEVITABLE?

In this section, I shall address the issue of why it should be thought that there are any concepts whose proper use is *inevitably* a matter of endless dispute. Essential contestability theses promise an expla-

[28] Raz, *The Morality of Freedom*, p. 326.

nation for the intractability of disputes over the proper application of central political concepts, not only in academic contexts but also outside of them. Gallie's proposed explanation appears to take the following form. Key political concepts such as 'democracy' and 'social justice' are essentially contested. They accredit a complex, valued achievement. Different elements in this achievement may be weighted differently by different contestants. New uses are generated by attaching different weights to these elements. Once a new use is introduced, it will inevitably find supporters who will defend it against those uses proposed by others. No proof can be given that one use is better than another and a person may reasonably continue to apply an essentially contested concept in a particular way in the face of counter arguments that have a 'definite logical force'.[29] As a result disagreement is 'natural' or 'humanly "likely"'.[30]

Consider an initial objection to this explanation which, although superficial, helps to clarify what is being proposed. Moral and political debate is possible only if the formation and expression of different moral and political opinions are permitted. So no concept can be *essentially* contested, since whether it is contested will depend on the existence of specific social and political conditions. This objection can be rebutted by making a distinction between the claim that a concept is essentially contes*ted* and the claim that it is essentially contes*table*. Gallie's thesis can then be stated in the following way: some social and political concepts are essentially contestable because their very *nature* makes the proper interpretation of them open to dispute, but will be essentially contested only if social and political conditions permit people to dispute their use. These conditions will include not only some measure of freedom of expression, but also whatever conditions are required to enable people 'to think for themselves', i.e. to be at least partially autonomous in judgement. We should also go further and acknowledge that a concept may be essentially contestable but uncontested in specific historical conditions that nevertheless permit it to be contested because those who engage in political debate do not regard it as important to dispute its use.[31] Terence Ball makes this point well:

[29] ECC, p. 190; PHU, p. 158.
[30] ECC, p. 176; p. 193. PHU, p. 165; p. 188.
[31] Gallie supposes, however, that under these circumstances essentially contestable concepts will *as a rule* be contested: see ECC, p. 169.

Not all concepts have been, or could be, contested at all times ... Conceptual contestation remains a permanent possibility even though it is, in practice, actualized only intermittently. The now-ubiquitous disputes about the meaning of 'democracy', for instance, are of relatively recent vintage, while the once-heated arguments about 'republic' have cooled considerably since the late 18th century ... Which concepts are believed to be worth disputing and revising is more often a political rather than a philosophical matter.[32]

Ball concludes from this that 'the language of political discourse is essentially contestable but the concepts comprising any political language are contingently contestable'. It seems to me, however, that we should conclude instead that a concept may be essentially contestable even when it is not actually contested; it may be that a concept is essentially contest*ed* during one period but not in another, even though it is essentially contest*able* the whole time.

This general explanation for the existence and persistence of political disagreement comes in two very different versions, however, depending on how we view the mechanisms which generate different moral and political beliefs. These versions are not distinguished by advocates of the thesis that key political concepts are essentially contested and it is often difficult to tell which they accept. Neither of them is purely a priori; both include an empirical component. In order to contrast them, we need to distinguish between rational and non-rational explanations for why beliefs are held. A *rational explanation* for why a person holds a belief cites only her reasons for doing so; a *non-rational explanation* cites only considerations other than reasons. Let me also stipulate that a belief is *rationally held* if a person holds it because of the reasons she has for thinking that it is true and no (other) causes are involved; a belief is non-rationally held if a person holds it because of causes other than reasons.[33] A belief may be rationally held even if it was not *initially* rationally caused. A person may accept a belief because, for example, she seeks the approval of others who hold it, but later on she may come to hold it because of her reasons for thinking that it is true. Even though for convenience I refer to reasons as causes, I mean to leave it an open question whether reasons can be causes of beliefs in the *same sense* that, say, sparks can be causes of explosions. The way in which a person's reasons explain why she holds her

[32] Ball, *Transforming Political Discourse*, p. 14.
[33] Cf. J. Elster, *Making Sense of Marx* (Cambridge: Cambridge University Press, 1985), p. 474.

beliefs may be completely different from the way in which a spark explains an explosion.

The two explanations for the existence and intractability of political disagreements distinguished earlier can now be stated as follows:

(1) When there is some measure of freedom of thought and expression, political disagreement will emerge because different uses of a number of political concepts are reasonable and, under these circumstances, there will be a diversity of rational causes of political belief formation.

(2) When there is some measure of freedom of thought and expression, political disagreement will emerge because different uses of a number of political concepts are reasonable and, under these circumstances, there will be a diversity of rational *and* non-rational causes of political belief formation.

(1) is a purely rational explanation. When rational explanations are thought to exhaust accounts of why people hold their moral and political beliefs, then the implication seems to be that they hold these beliefs solely because of the reasons they have for thinking that they are true, i.e. that they are fully autonomous in judgement. But in the face of evidence from disciplines such as psychology, sociology and politics, it is hard to believe that, for example, people in developed capitalist societies are, on the whole, fully autonomous in judgement, even if we regard this as an ideal to which people should aspire. So version (2) is the most plausible thesis because only it is compatible with empirical findings. It encourages us to *integrate* rational and non-rational explanations for the holding of beliefs: when we explain people's allegiances we should cite their reasons for using terms in the ways they do and make reference to any sociological and psychological causes for why they find some considerations salient, i.e. for why some considerations are perceived as compelling reasons by them.

It is crucial to recognize the different possible empirical components of the thesis that key social and political concepts are essentially contested, distinguished in (1) and (2). If we do not, we risk confusing two distinct issues: the question of what is at issue between those who apply social and political terms differently (the answer to which lies 'in the space of reasons') and the question of why people apply these terms differently (the answer to which may or may not lie 'in the space of reasons'). To assume that when we know what is at issue between people who disagree in their use of terms, we know why they disagree is to be blind to the possible relevance of psychological and sociological investigation in this area. Which of (1) and (2) does Gallie accept? I think he accepts (2) because while insisting that people favour different uses of essentially contested concepts at least partly because they attach different weights to competing considerations, he also claims that 'at any given stage in the history of an essentially contested concept, it will be no doubt necessary to call upon psychological or sociological history or the known historical facts of a person's or group's backgrounds, to explain their present preferences and adherences'.[34]

The idea that political disagreement exists and will persist provided certain minimal conditions continue to be met, which is implicit in both (1) and (2), is controversial. According to an interpretation that is widely accepted (but is nevertheless controversial), Marx argued that political disagreement would disappear with the abolition of private property and the emergence of new forms of consciousness that would follow from collective control of the means of production. On this reading, although Marx believed that political disagreement would be insignificant as long as capitalist society continued to maximize the development of the productive forces, he thought that when radical criticisms of that social order began to emerge, the implicit and explicit disagreement that ensued would be transitory and disappear when capitalism was fully transcended, for two sorts of reasons. Firstly, juridical concepts, such as concepts of justice and human rights, only have a role in societies in which there is a shortage of goods and in which people are antagonistic towards each other. In communist society, in which production will be brought under collective rational control, there will be abundance of goods and any initial disputes about how goods are to be distributed will be resolvable without recourse to prescriptive rules because people will share a common interest, be co-operative and willing to compromise.[35] Secondly, capitalist society has a

---

[34] ECC, p. 192; PHU, p. 187. I suspect that Gallie endorses (b) for the wrong reasons, however, since he appears to think that if people attach different weights to different considerations, there *must* be a non-rational explanation for why they do so: 'fundamental differences of attitude, of a kind for which no logical justification can be given, must also lie at the back [of disputes over essentially contested concepts]' (ECC, p. 191; PHU, p. 186). But why is a non-rational explanation logically required here? It is coherent to maintain that rational explanations exhaust the account of why people disagree over the proper use of a term; the question is whether as a matter of fact they do provide complete explanations.

[35] See, e.g. S. Lukes, *Marxism and Morality* (Oxford: Oxford University Press, 1985); A. E. Buchanan, *Marx and Justice: The Radical Critique of Liberalism* (London: Methuen, 1982).

misleading superficial appearance that tends to generate false beliefs about it. In contrast, in communist society where superficial appearance and reality will coincide, the social world will be transparent and judgements using non-juridical political terms such as 'freedom' and 'power' will be undisputed.[36]

There are several difficulties with the Marxian challenge thus understood, however. Firstly, the belief that technology and collective control together would generate such an abundance of goods that distributive questions would become either less troublesome or non-existent appears optimistic, to say the least. Secondly, the appearance/reality distinction that Marx exploits in claiming that capitalism has a misleading superficial form is problematic. Marx appeals to examples from the non-human world in order to support it: air appears to be elementary but science reveals that it is composite; the sun appears to rise, but science tells us that it is the earth that moves, not the sun.[37] However, as contemporary philosophers of science have made us aware, the way the world appears to us depends very much on the kind of theories we bring to it.[38] This point can be made just as forcefully with respect to the social world. As Steven Lukes has emphasized, whether we see exercises of power, or whether we are blind to them, is strongly influenced by the theoretical perspectives we occupy. If we believe that power is exercised only when someone's desires are thwarted, we will fail to see the exercises of power which are involved in manipulating desires so that they do not coincide with a person's real interests.[39] The same is true of restrictions of freedom: if we believe that only obstacles which are intentionally imposed can restrict freedom, we will fail to see the way in which the unintentional consequences of a person's actions can restrict another's freedom.[40]

This reading of Marx has been seriously challenged, however: see, e.g. N. Geras, 'Seven Types of Obloquy: Travesties of Marxism', *Socialist Register*, 1990, especially parts II and VI.

[36] See G. A. Cohen, *Karl Marx's Theory of History: A Defence* (Princeton, NJ: Princeton University Press, 1978), appendix I.

[37] K. Marx, *Capital*, vol. 1 (Moscow, 1961), p. 316; p. 74. (Cited by G. A. Cohen, *Karl Marx's Theory of History*, p. 327.)

[38] Hanson and Kuhn first brought home the importance of this idea, which is now generally accepted by philosophers of science (even though it is not thought to have the radical implications that, e.g. Kuhn imagined): see T. Kuhn, *The Structure of Scientific Revolutions* second edition (Chicago, IL: University of Chicago Press, 1970); N. Hanson, *Patterns of Discovery: An Inquiry into the Conceptual Foundations of Science* (Cambridge: Cambridge University Press, 1958).

[39] See Lukes, *Power*.

[40] See D. Miller, 'Constraints on Freedom'.

Thirdly, and most importantly, even if disagreement in developed capitalist societies is rooted in the scarcity of goods and the antagonistic nature of the relationships between people, it does not follow that abundance and transformation of these relationships will eliminate all forms of recognizably political disagreement, e.g. about how power should be distributed and decisions made. Even if people would be fully autonomous in communist society and their beliefs entirely rationally caused, there might still be scope for reasonable disagreement on moral and political matters and the existence of disagreement might be accounted for simply by citing the reasons people have for disagreeing. This point applies quite generally, and is independent of the details of Marx's account; radicals should leave it an open question whether disagreement would ensue in social and political orders in which people were fully autonomous in judgement.

This criticism perhaps also applies to some of Jürgen Habermas's work. Habermas claims that the structure of potential (and actual) speech presupposes a set of rules for constructing an 'ideal speech situation'.[41] This ideal speech situation 'is neither an empirical phenomenon, nor simply a construct, but a required supposition unavoidable in discourse'.[42] This supposition can be expressed counterfactually, as a set of conditions that are required for any consensus that is reached to be rational or genuine, rather than forced. These conditions are, for instance, that all participants in the debate from which the consensus emerges must have equal power (i.e. must be free from all forms of domination) and that unlimited discussion must be possible. Habermas's account seems to imply that under these conditions not only is any consensus that arises genuine, but also that a rational moral and political consensus would follow. The second of these claims seems to be entailed by two other views Habermas defends: firstly, that 'practical questions admit of truth',[43] and secondly, that truth 'can only be analysed with regard to a consensus achieved in unrestrained and universal discourse'.[44] If truth is (roughly speaking) uncoerced consensus and moral and

---

[41] See Habermas, 'Towards a Theory of Communicative Competence', *Inquiry*, vol. 13, 1970, p. 372.

[42] J. Habermas, 'Wahrheitstheorien' in *Wirklichkeit und Reflexion: Walter Schultz zum 60. Geburtstag* ed H. Fahrenbach (Pfullingen: Neske, 1973), p. 258. (Translated and quoted by T. McCarthy in his introduction to J. Habermas, *Legitimation Crisis* (London: Heinemann, 1976), p. xvii.)

[43] Habermas, *Legitimation Crisis*, p. 111.

[44] Habermas, 'Towards a Theory of Communicative Competence', p. 327.

political judgements have truth values, then in an ideal speech situation a rational moral and political consensus would emerge. If this is a correct interpretation of Habermas's account, it is vulnerable to the criticism that even if people were fully autonomous in judgement, they might have reasons for making different moral and political judgements and because of these reasons they might disagree with each other.

Habermas's account does allow for a degree of disagreement in the ideal speech situation, which might seem to make possible a reconciliation of it with essential contestedness theses. In the ideal speech situation, the 'formal properties of discourse and of the deliberative situation sufficiently guarantee that a consensus can arise only through appropriately interpreted, *generalizable* interests'.[45] This implies that (in the absence of compromise) *only* practical judgements which express common interests will be agreed upon there and hence, presumably, only practical judgements that express common interests have truth values. So Habermas's account can allow for considerable moral and political disagreement even if the conditions that govern the ideal speech situation were realized. However, if Habermas is to claim that a significant range of practical judgements have truth values (as indeed he seems to), he must I think deny the thesis that central social and political concepts (such as the concept of social justice) are essentially contested, for if they were essentially contested then (according to defenders of that thesis) convergence on any significant range of practical judgements would not arise even in an ideal speech situation.

4 SOME QUALIFICATIONS

In the previous sections, I have clarified essential contestedness theses and defended them against some objections which critics have thought to be decisive. In this final section, I propose to qualify some of the claims made by them in order to answer some further doubts that might be expressed about the role they play in explaining the intractability of contemporary moral and political disagreement.

The thesis that key moral and political concepts are essentially contested, as I have interpreted it, maintains that when there is some measure of freedom of thought and expression, moral and

[45] Habermas, *Legitimation Crisis*, p. 108; see p. 110.

political disagreement will inevitably emerge (even though for historically specific reasons people may not actually contest particular concepts which are open to dispute). That idea can be questioned by examining the role of two other contingent features of moral and political discourse in making possible, and helping to explain, the extensiveness and persistence of contemporary moral and political disagreement.

Paul Seabright draws attention to the way in which different disciplines[46] take a different attitude towards the achievement of consensus. He observes that not all disciplines aim at consensus and amongst those that do aim at consensus, the importance of this goal in relation to other goals may differ.[47] He suggests that different degrees of convergence in different disciplines, or areas of discourse, can be explained in terms of the different priority given to consensus by their practitioners. Practitioners of a discipline may not aim to reach agreement; they may, for example, merely try to clarify their own position by pitting it against others and by noting its points of divergence with them. If they do aim to reach consensus, this aim may be secondary to others, such as the discovery of truth. Seabright suggests that, for instance, the natural sciences and ethics differ with respect to how they view consensus as a goal in relation to others: in the natural sciences consensus is regarded as more important than it is in ethics and politics, where elimination of disagreement although regarded as desirable, is not pursued so single-mindedly. This difference in the aims of disciplines is at least partially responsible for the different degrees of convergence in them. If Seabright is correct, then the training natural scientists receive socializes them to give consensus a different priority from that it has in moral and political thought.

It does not follow that if the pursuit of *consensus* is given less priority in ethics/politics than in the natural sciences, then the same must be true of *persuasion*. Practitioners of a discipline may aim to persuade without aiming at consensus: if a person genuinely aims at consensus, she must recognize that she may have to concede that she was mistaken, or (if appropriate) give up her proposal, whereas if she merely aims to persuade others to accept her (present) view, she

---

[46] Although Seabright talks of disciplines, it is clear that he doesn't mean to restrict the scope of his remarks to the *professional* practice of them.

[47] See P. Seabright, 'Objectivity, Disagreement, and Projectability', *Inquiry*, vol. 31, 1988, pp. 25–51.

cannot allow this possibility in so far as she does so single-mindedly. So we could concede that emotivists such as Stevenson were correct in thinking that persuasion was a fundamental goal of moral and political discourse even if we deny that consensus is so as well.

The second feature which might play a role in explaining different degrees of convergence in different areas that is independent of the scope for reasonable disagreement in them is identified by Sabina Lovibond. She argues that different disciplines give different scope to 'intellectual authority' and that the different reach of intellectual authority in different disciplines can explain the different amounts of agreement and disagreement to be found in them.

Our induction into a form of life involves an ultimately coercive process of socialization in which we are taught to use terms, including moral and political ones, correctly. Children (and those who have not yet become competent speakers in some sphere of discourse) are in the final analysis forced to recognize the authority of others on how terms should be used. This process of socialization occurs in all areas of discourse; however, the reach of intellectual authority varies from one area to another and can explain different degrees of convergence in different disciplines. Lovibond argues that in the natural sciences generally only a small latitude of disagreement with acknowledged authorities is allowed before those who challenge received views are regarded as incompetent users of terms and are corrected.[48] In the natural sciences, 'any mild deviations from consensus (except, presumably, at the frontiers of our knowledge) are liable to result, by common consent, in forfeiture of one's right to participate in the game'.[49] In ethics and politics, although some uses of terms which go against received views will be regarded as deviant, a considerable amount of 'legitimate' disagreement is acknowledged: disputants will still be regarded as competent speakers, albeit ones with mistaken views, i.e. they will be regarded as making applications of moral and political terms that are sufficiently reasonable not to be dismissed as simply deviant. As I interpret it, this is a purely factual claim about moral and political discourse: it is not equivalent to the normative claim that disputants *do* make reasonable applications of moral and political terms, which is the idea invoked by essential contestedness theses.

Note that the reach of intellectual authority may be lengthened

[48] See Lovibond, *Realism and Imagination*, especially sections 15 and 17.
[49] *Ibid.*, p. 67.

without restrictions being placed on freedom of expression. Although treating people's use of political terms as deviant may have the effect of silencing them, it does not necessarily involve restricting their freedom to express different opinions. It might be plausibly argued, however, that when the reach of intellectual authority becomes so long that reasonable opinions are dismissed as deviant uses of terms, then it does involve a restriction on freedom of expression. Complete freedom of expression is preserved only when reasonable political viewpoints are *regarded* as reasonable enough not to be dismissed as simply a misuse of the terms used to express them.

Lovibond understands the short reach of intellectual authority to be a contingent fact about modern moral discourse: it is a description of how speakers in, for example, capitalist societies apply moral terms and correct others' use of these terms. As she acknowledges, it does not represent a universal truth: the reach of intellectual authority in ethics has varied throughout history and between societies. It is possible to imagine societies (or perhaps describe actual societies) in which the reach of intellectual authority on ethical and political matters was far greater than in developed capitalist societies, and in which any non-standard uses of political terms were simply regarded as deviant and corrected. The different reach intellectual authority in ethics and politics has in some societies compared to others stands in need of explanation, but not an a priori one in terms of differences in kinds of reasoning.

The contingent features of contemporary moral and political discourse highlighted by Lovibond and Seabright suggest that moral and political disagreement would not inevitably occur whenever there was some degree of freedom of thought and expression. People may be socialized into striving for consensus on moral and political questions without restricting their freedom of thought and expression; if reaching consensus was a primary aim of moral and political discourse, then people might come to agree on moral and political matters even though reasonable disagreement was still possible. If the reach of intellectual authority were lengthened without restricting freedom of thought and expression, this would nevertheless produce greater convergence on moral and political issues. The role of consensus amongst the aims of moral and political discourse, and the short reach of intellectual authority on moral and political questions, make possible moral and political disagreement and help to explain why it is so intractable.

There is another, related worry about essential contestedness theses which concerns their scope: how much moral and political disagreement can they play a role in explaining? Not all applications of moral and political concepts are reasonable; some are simply mistaken. Why suppose that in all cases of intractable moral and political dispute, the viewpoints involved are reasonable? Perhaps in some important cases the persistence of a disagreement could be explained *simply* by contingent features of contemporary moral and political discourse: for instance, the presence of some freedom of thought and expression, the relatively weak priority given to achieving consensus in moral and political debate, and the reach of intellectual authority within it. We cannot justifiably rule out this possibility a priori; there is no way of telling a priori how much political disagreement is partially explicable in terms of the idea that it concerns an issue over which reasonable disagreement is possible.

I have maintained that the idea central to essential contestedness theses, that different uses of key moral and political concepts are reasonable, has an important role to play in explaining the intractability of moral and political disagreement. In doing so I have endorsed an element of the contestability conception of how moral and political disagreement is to be explained. But I have accepted an element of the imperfection conception as well because I have defended the idea that even when disputes are not resolvable to the satisfaction of every reasonable person who has the time and interest to think through the issues, and who is fully competent in applying the laws of logic, there may nevertheless be a correct answer to them which requires 'judgement' to discern. In this final section I have also qualified the thesis that key political concepts are essentially contested by arguing that contingent features of moral and political discourse are significant in explaining the intractability of moral and political disagreement. In the next chapter, I turn to an objection to essential contestedness theses which is itself employed as part of an explanation of why political disputes are so persistent: the idea that key political terms are used to express different concepts, not just different conceptions of the same concept, and that those who dispute their proper use simply talk past each other.

CHAPTER 3

The miscommunication thesis

The thesis that key political concepts are essentially contested, a qualified version of which I defended in the last chapter, maintains that disputants employ the same concepts but interpret them differently. That belief stands in need of justification, however, for it has been argued that people disagree on political matters precisely because they *lack* shared concepts. According to this position, those who disagree politically employ key terms to express different concepts and in consequence simply talk past each other; they are not involved in genuine disagreements at all.

This general view, which I shall call *the miscommunication thesis*, comes in different versions. In some versions, the explanation it provides for the fact of political disagreement fits the imperfection conception, since it allows the possibility that miscommunication can be avoided through more careful use of language. For example, Locke argues that moral and political disputes are largely due to the misuse of words: people use different terms to stand for the same idea, and the same term to stand for different ideas. He claims that provided we are clear about which ideas our moral terms signify, disagreements can be cleared up to the satisfaction of any reasonable person and we can gain true moral knowledge. I shall discuss Locke's view further in section 1. In section 2, I consider a related account which differs from Locke's in that it does not presuppose his theory of language and communication. Some other versions of the miscommunication thesis hold that misunderstanding is irremovable. These fit the contestability conception of how political disagreement is to be explained, for they maintain that rationally irresolvable confrontations between different moral and political frameworks are inevitable. Thomas Kuhn's work in the philosophy of science has facilitated this kind of account of the nature of moral and political disagreement, which I shall discuss in section 3.

The idea that there is a failure of communication between adherents to rival political positions has some plausibility. Although there may be agreement on the application of key political terms to a range of cases, there is nevertheless significant disagreement, often over what are considered to be *central* applications.[1] People disagree over which applications are the primary, most important ones for the understanding and assessment of political activities, relations and institutions, and sometimes one person will also deny that the applications another regards as central are even legitimate. Consider disagreements over the application of one key political expression, 'exercising power over'. The dominant liberal analysis is bound up with the notions of intention and preference: A exercises power over B when A intentionally brings it about that B does something that B doesn't want to do. In contrast, the radical view developed at a theoretical level by Steven Lukes separates the exercise of power from agents' intentions and, furthermore, links it to real interests rather than wants: A exercises power over B if, and only if, A affects B in a manner contrary to B's real interests.[2] Radicals might hold that a wife who willingly but with great self-sacrifice meets her husband's emotional and sexual needs is compliant because he exercises power over her, even when they would not contend that he does so consciously. Some radical feminists would argue that there are central cases like this in which men exercise power over women, for they believe that heterosexuality is a compulsory institution with marriage its dominant form.[3] For a liberal, however, this sort of analysis misconceives what it is for one person to exercise power over another; the liberal's paradigmatic example is the thief who acquires a wallet at gunpoint, and they understand other exercises of power on this model.

Consider also disputes over whether a person is free or unfree. Liberals and so-called 'libertarians' have often defined freedom as the absence of coercion, i.e. the absence of intentional restrictions on choice. In consequence they have not regarded poverty, when it does not arise from coercion, as a restriction on freedom. Socialists, in contrast, have generally thought that a person's freedom may be

---

[1] See, e.g. D. Miller, 'Linguistic Philosophy and Political Theory', pp. 41ff. and J. Gray, 'Political Power, Social Theory and Essential Contestability', p. 95, in D. Miller and L. Siedentop (eds), *The Nature of Political Theory* (Oxford: Oxford University Press, 1983).

[2] See Lukes, *Power*.

[3] See A. Rich, 'Compulsory Heterosexuality and Lesbian Existence' in A. Snitow, C. Stansell and S. Thompson (eds) *Desire: The Politics of Sexuality* (London: Virago, 1984).

restricted even when she has not been coerced: a person may be unfree to do something when her inability to do it is the unintended result of human agency. For many socialists, central cases of unfreedom are to be found where people suffer from poverty that is the unintended consequence of market transactions. A socialist is likely to regard these cases as central because they provide an important part of the explanation for why she does not consider 'the free market' to be a system of pure or complete freedom in the way that libertarians tend to do.

The idea that people who occupy very different political positions talk past each other receives further support from another observation: disagreements over the proper use of one key political term are related to (and sometimes spill over into) disagreements over the proper use of others. Consider again the expression 'exercises power over'. Disagreements over the use of this expression are sometimes connected to disagreements over the use of the term 'interests'. Superficial agreement that A exercises power when A significantly affects B's interests can mask substantive disagreement over what constitutes 'significantly affecting a person's interests'. Liberals standardly assume that there is an intimate relationship between interests and desires or preferences. In its crudest form, this relationship is held to be such that if A prevents B from satisfying one of his (B's) desires, then A has set back B's interests, whereas on the other hand, if B has no desire to do x, then A cannot have damaged B's interests in making it impossible for B to do x. In contrast radicals leave open the possibility that a person's interests may be set back despite the fact that none of her actual desires have been thwarted. More sophisticated accounts of the connection between a person's interests and their desires or preferences are available within liberalism,[4] but as a generalization we can say that differences over what counts as an exercise of power are often mirrored by differences over what constitutes a person's interests, for even on these more sophisticated accounts a person can be mistaken about her interests only in so far as she is wrong about the necessary or best means for realizing her deepest desires and projects: interests are conceived roughly as *informed* desires or preferences.

David Miller's claim that liberals and socialists often disagree over what counts as an instance of unfreedom because they disagree

---

[4] See, e.g. J. Feinberg's desire-based account of interests in *The Moral Limits of the Criminal Law, Vol. 1: Harm to Others* (New York: Oxford University Press, 1984).

over questions of moral responsibility perhaps highlights a further case in which one dispute precipitates another. If he is correct, then differences over whether the poverty which is an unintended but foreseeable result of market transactions makes people who suffer from it unfree, or merely unable to do various things that are beyond their means, rest in part on differences over whether anyone can properly be held morally responsible for that poverty. In his view, disputes between liberals and socialists over this issue may (and sometimes should) lead to disputes over our *prima facie* moral obligations to others, for these obligations determine our moral responsibilities.

Disputes do not therefore involve isolated concepts: particular concepts are embedded in a network of relationships with each other and disputes over the proper use of one concept have a tendency to precipitate disagreement over the proper use of a range of related concepts. The systematic, inter-connected nature of political disputes, and the way in which superficial agreement can mask substantive disagreement, encourages the view that those who engage in these disputes fail to understand each other. That conclusion seems to be forced upon us if we also accept a particular view of the conditions under which meaningful disagreement is possible, viz. the view that disagreements are genuine only if disputants share roughly the same criteria for applying terms. When people disagree fundamentally over the proper use of terms, it seems that they cannot share criteria for applying them. On the conception of meaningful disagreement just described it would appear to follow that disputes between them could not be genuine:[5] those who challenge radically the applications others make of key political terms will fail to communicate with those they criticize.

I THE LOCKEAN EXPLANATION[6]

My concern is with the use of the idea that people who disagree over the proper application of political terms fail to understand each

---

[5] See, e.g. S. Hampshire, *Thought and Action* (London: Chatto and Windus, 1959), p. 229 for an expression of this position. R. Dworkin discusses it in *Law's Empire*, pp. 45ff. Some seem to hold an even stronger view about the relation between successful communication and agreement: Russell Keat suggests that Habermas believes successful communication must involve, or produce, agreement (see R. Keat, *The Politics of Social Theory* (Oxford: Blackwell, 1981), pp. 195–6).

[6] This section is adapted from my 'Locke on Disagreement Over the Use of Moral and Political Terms', *The Locke Newsletter*, vol. 20, 1989, pp. 63–75, which pays greater scholarly attention to the details of Locke's argument.

other in order to *explain* why these disputes are so pervasive and intractable. I shall begin with a classic example: the version presented by John Locke in Book III of *An Essay Concerning Human Understanding*.

On Locke's account of the nature of language, language performs two roles: firstly, it allows us to record our own thoughts as an aid to recollection and, secondly, it enables us to communicate our thoughts to others.[7] Words acquire their meaning by, and in virtue of, signifying ideas. They directly signify the ideas of the person who uses them,[8] but when language functions properly as a means of communication, they excite the same ideas in others. Moral ideas are especially difficult to communicate effectively because they are complex in two respects: they are constructed out of *several* of the simple ideas which the mind receives passively in experience, and the simple ideas that are utilized are of *diverse* kinds.[9] Unlike terms which signify simple ideas, however, it is hard to give moral terms a settled and precise signification for they cannot be defined by pure ostension; in order to define moral terms precisely, the ideas for which they stand have to be broken down into their constituent parts until simple ideas are reached which may then be defined by ostension. Moral terms not only tend to stand for different ideas from one person to another, but also their signification within a single mind is often not settled or precise.[10]

This natural tendency towards misunderstanding is aggravated because ordinarily people do not conscientiously strive to give precise definitions to moral terms. But Locke is optimistic about the possibility of clearing up confusions by philosophical analysis – the purpose of which is to attain knowledge – even though he doubts whether the same clarity could ever be achieved in civil discourse, i.e. 'common conversation and commerce about the ordinary affairs and conveniences of civil life'.[11] Indeed he maintains that definitions of moral terms give us certain knowledge of the meaning of these

---

[7] J. Locke, *An Essay Concerning Human Understanding* (New York: Dover, 1959) (hereafter referred to as *Essay*), vol. II, book III, ix, 1.

[8] *Ibid.*, III, ii, 2.

[9] In Locke's view, moral ideas are also difficult to keep track of because they do not correspond to real existences in nature: see *Essay*, III, ix, 7.

[10] Locke, *Essay*, III, ix, 6.

[11] He expresses his pessimism about the possibility of eliminating confusion in the civil use of words when he says: 'I am not so vain as to think that any one can pretend to attempt the perfect reforming of the languages of the world, no not so much as of his own country, without rendering himself ridiculous' (*Essay*, III, xi, 2).

terms 'without leaving any room for any contest about it'.[12] In Locke's view 'morality is capable of demonstration, as well as mathematics'.[13]

Locke's optimism concerning the possibility of resolving disputes over the application of moral and political terms by philosophical analysis has been misplaced since disagreement has strongly persisted even within moral and political philosophy. That is not enough to refute his account, however, for he might respond by arguing that getting clear on which ideas our moral terms signify has proved even more difficult than he envisaged. The strongest challenge to Locke's account focuses instead on his theory of language and communication and has its source in Wittgenstein's writings. Wittgenstein's discussion of meaning offers perhaps the most sustained attack on Locke's conception of language; this is true despite the fact that Wittgenstein never mentions Locke by name and probably didn't have him specifically in mind when he was writing. Wittgenstein's criticisms also apply to other structurally similar theories of language and communication, such as Hobbes's account[14] and the account Bentham favoured in his early writings.[15] Although Hobbes's explanation for why people disagree in their use of terms such as 'justice' runs parallel to Locke's in several respects, it has at least one important difference from it. According to Hobbes, moral terms have an 'inconstant signification', i.e. are used by people to signify different 'conceptions', because their use is partly governed by the *attitudes* of the speaker:

For though the nature of that we conceive, be the same; yet the diversity of our reception of it, in respect of different constitutions of body, and prejudices of opinion, gives everything a tincture of different passions ... For one man calleth *Wisdome*, what another calleth *feare*; and one *cruelty*, what another *justice* ...[16]

So Hobbes, unlike Locke, appears to endorse a version of the contestability conception.

The theory of how language functions with which we are con-

---

[12] Locke, *Essay*, III, xi, 17.
[13] *Ibid.*, III, xi, 16.
[14] See T. Hobbes, *Leviathan* (ed) C. B. Macpherson (Harmondsworth, Middlesex: Penguin, 1968), pt. 1, ch. 4.
[15] See J. Bentham, *A Comment on the Commentaries and A Fragment on Government* (ed) J. H. Burns and H. L. A. Hart (London: Athlone, 1977), p. 347. Bentham seems to present a different kind of account in his later writings, however.
[16] Hobbes, *Leviathan*, p. 109.

cerned, and which Locke's account exemplifies, assumes that if a term is meaningful, it must stand for some idea which determines how it should be used. In several passages in the *Philosophical Investigations*, Wittgenstein is concerned to undermine a view of this kind. As I understand it, the implication of his argument is that if ideas were images, *or analogous to images*, they could not determine what it is to use the terms which stand for them correctly.[17] Images are susceptible to diverse interpretations and do not themselves determine which of these interpretations is the correct one, i.e. they are not *self*-interpreting. Think of the idea of a cube. If this idea is constituted by the image of a cube (or something analogous), that image can be 'projected' differently:

> suppose that a picture does come before your mind when you hear the word 'cube', say the drawing of a cube. In what sense can this picture fit or fail to fit a use of the word 'cube'? – Perhaps you say: 'It's quite simple; – if that picture occurs to me and I point to a triangular prism for instance, and say it is a cube, then this use of the word doesn't fit the picture.' – But doesn't it fit? I have purposely chosen the example so that it is quite easy to imagine a *method of projection* according to which the picture does fit after all.
>
> The picture of the cube did indeed *suggest* a certain use to us, but it was possible for me to use it differently.[18]

There is nothing *in* the image of the cube which determines its correct method of projection.[19] But, it might be thought, couldn't a Lockean idea of a cube be made up of an image (or something analogous) *together with* the rules for projecting the image, so that these jointly determine how the word 'cube' is to be used? As Wittgenstein points out, however, any representation of a method of projection can itself be variously interpreted:

> Perhaps I see before me a schema showing the method of projection: say a picture of two cubes connected by lines of projection. – But does this really get me any further? Can't I now imagine different applications of this schema too?[20]

Positing that rules of projection, together with a mental picture, constitute a Lockean idea cannot explain how the application of a term which stands for that idea is determined. A Lockean might

---

[17] See PI, especially sections 72–4, 139–141; L. Wittgenstein, *The Blue and Brown Books* (Oxford: Blackwell, 1960), especially pp. 1–6, 12–17.

[18] PI, section 139.

[19] Cf. also Wittgenstein, *The Blue and Brown Books*, p. 33.

[20] PI, section 141.

simply assert that 'ideas' are disanalogous to images or pictures and do determine the correct applications of the terms which stand for them. But in the absence of any account of *how* they determine the correct application of these terms, such a claim verges on incoherence. It presupposes that there is a mental act of understanding – in Locke's terms, 'having an idea' – which contains within it the correct applications of a sign as if 'in a *queer* way, the use itself is in some sense present'.[21]

Even if we were to grant Locke the thesis that ideas determine the correct application of the terms which stand for them, his account of how we succeed in communicating the ideas we have in our heads to others would have further problems. On Locke's account, we can communicate because we are capable of having the same kind of mental entity (i.e. the same kind of idea) and using the same term to stand for it. As Locke himself recognized (and exploited in his explanation of why we disagree over the application of moral and political terms), on the view of language he presents we might misunderstand each other because we use the same word to signify different ideas. But even if we accept that there is some set of ideas in our heads which our terms signify, which determine the correct application of these terms in all contexts, on Locke's account there is no guarantee that misunderstandings of this kind can be cleared up by giving a different description of an idea, for this *new* description might not signify the same idea in each of our languages.

A Lockean might appeal to his account of how complex moral ideas are built up from simple ideas and argue that we can ensure communication by analyzing these ideas into their constituents until we reach simple ideas, which are unambiguously definable by ostension. This was Locke's suggestion for how we should clear up disputes over the application of terms that stand for moral ideas. But any ostensive definition can be variously interpreted.[22] There is no act of pointing that will necessarily individuate a unique simple idea and serve to anchor our terms so as to secure a shared language. For example, if a person tried to define 'red' by pointing to a red truck, this act of pointing might be taken to refer to the truck, its shape, its size, or what it's made of. The presentation of more cases to which the term 'red' can be correctly applied is equally vulnerable to

[21] PI, section 195. See also PI, sections 187–97.
[22] See PI, section 28.

diverse interpretations, regardless of whether these cases are homogeneous or heterogeneous.

If we did use our terms to stand for different ideas, we might have no way knowing. Even if we agree in our application of a term to a range of cases, this does not demonstrate that we are using it to stand for the same idea. We might 'agree' in our applications of a term yet fail to communicate because it does not signify the same idea in each of our languages, since different ideas can generate the same applications across any finite range of cases. So the mere fact that we have agreed in our judgements in the past is consistent with our grasping a different Lockean idea since the past usage of a word will always be compatible with that word standing for a variety of different Lockean ideas. This is comparable to the way that any series of numbers is compatible with a variety of different algebraic formulae.[23] Furthermore, contexts might never arise in the future which would enable persons to realize that they do use a term to signify different ideas. On Locke's theory, whether we *ever* use the same words to stand for the same ideas will always be open to doubt.

Wittgenstein's criticisms of the kind of model of language and communication that Locke advocates are not in my view intended to raise sceptical doubts about whether we do ever mean the same thing, or do ever follow the same rules in applying a linguistic expression (see chapter 1, section 3): their point is rather to cast doubt on the very conception of meaning and understanding presupposed by it. The fact that the Lockean account of how communication works leaves open the possibility that we might always fail to understand each other (even when we think we succeed in doing so) is not itself a refutation of it. Perhaps a Lockean could allow this possibility without being forced to accept the sceptical conclusion that we have no grounds for thinking that we do ever communicate if he could argue that the best explanation of why we agree in our use of terms (when we do) is that we employ them to stand for the same ideas. But in the light of the earlier criticism that ideas do not even determine the correct application of the terms that stand for them, it is implausible to think that Locke's theory provides even part of the best explanation for how and why we sometimes succeed in communicating.

What conception of meaning and understanding (if any) Wittgenstein seeks to put in place of the kind of account that Locke and

---

23 Cf. PI, section 146.

others have endorsed is a matter of some dispute. Commentators apparently agree that Wittgenstein proposes that what an individual means by some term or expression is determined by the linguistic *practices* in which he or she participates, but disagree about the implications of this view, e.g. over whether it allows that an individual can mean anything at all in isolation from a community with shared practices. Putting aside these important issues, Wittgenstein's proposal seems to imply straightforwardly that people share the same concepts if, and only if, they are participants in the same practices.[24] Whether this view is defensible depends in part on what criteria govern the identity of a practice and hence how we are to decide that people are engaged in the same practices. What I go on to say in the sections which follow is broadly compatible with a Wittgensteinian account of this sort but does not presuppose one.

2 DIFFERENT CONCEPTS, DIFFERENT INTERPRETATIONS OF THE SAME CONCEPT AND GENUINE DISAGREEMENT

Even if the Lockean view that disagreements over the application of political terms result from different people using the same term to stand for different mental entities fails because of the theory of language and communication it presupposes, it may still be true that our central moral and political terms are ambiguous. So there is room for the argument that disputes between people over how to apply them correctly are in some respects analogous to a confusion displayed by two small children when one claims that a bank is a place where money is held, whilst the other insists that it is really a steep slope. If such a position is to be defensible, it cannot presuppose a Lockean theory of language and communication; however, it can (like the Lockean account of disagreement) allow for the possibility of communication between those who have different political standpoints, and it can hold that the proper way to go about rationally resolving disputes is to distinguish different senses of terms by using other terms which do have a shared meaning. An account of this sort would therefore provide another version of the imperfection conception of how political disagreement is to be explained.

One way of arguing against the idea that most of our central moral and political terms are ambiguous, and that in consequence

---

[24] See Hurley, *Natural Reasons*, ch. 3.

disputes over these terms are generally a result of simple miscommunication, would be to provide a criterion for distinguishing ambiguous terms from those that are univocal which shows that political terms in general are univocal. This is the strategy which defenders of the thesis that our central moral and political terms are essentially contested have followed in trying to establish that disagreements over the application of political terms are indeed genuine.

In Gallie's view, people disagree over the application of an essentially contested concept because they describe the achievement accredited by it differently. His account faces a challenge of which he is aware: how do we know that contestants aren't simply describing *different* achievements? As Gallie's imaginary objector puts it: 'the kind of situation ... described is indistinguishable from those situations in which people engage in apparently endless contests as to the right application of some epithet or slogan, which in fact serves to confuse two *different* concepts about whose proper application no one need have contested at all'.[25] In such a case the term is 'not essentially, but only accidentally and as a result of persistent confusion, mutually contesting and contested'.[26] This threat may appear to be defused by the fact that contestants use the same criteria for applying a particular essentially contested concept even though they disagree over how much weight to attach to each of them. In response Gallie's objector would point out that this may be insufficient for us to be able to determine whether disputants are describing the same achievement, because in practice it may be impossible to distinguish between a use of a term in which a person attaches considerable weight to one of a number of criteria which govern its application (call it C_1) and minimal weight to the others (C_2, C_3 and C_4), and a use of a term which has a single criterion (C_1) for its correct application. In the former case that use is one amongst (potentially) many uses of the shared concept which are generated by attaching greater weight to the other criteria (C_2, C_3 and C_4) and each is an expression of the same concept; in the latter case only one criterion governs the proper application of the term and hence the concept cannot be essentially contested by Gallie's lights.[27]

---

[25] ECC, p. 175; PHU, p. 163.
[26] ECC, p. 176; PHU, p. 164.
[27] It might be argued that nevertheless people share concepts only if they share criteria even if it can be impossible in practice to tell. Although sharing criteria may be a sufficient

Gallie proposed two extra conditions which he thought helped perform the task of separating genuine essentially contested concepts from ambiguous terms:[28] firstly, an essentially contested concept must be derived from an original exemplar whose authority is acknowledged by all the contestant users of the concept; secondly, continuous competition between rival users of the concept must make probable or plausible the claim that the original exemplar's achievement has been sustained or developed in optimum fashion.[29] Many commentators have understood the condition that an essentially contested concept must be derived from an original exemplar to amount to the requirement that there be some actual historical case which all contestants agree exemplifies the achievement accredited by the concept in question if it is to be correctly characterized as essentially contested.[30] But a condition that all contestants agree in their judgements on some actual case seems unjustifiably restrictive and it is unclear why it should be a requirement. Many political concepts will fail to meet it. David Miller notes that two of Gallie's own examples, democracy and social justice do not satisfy it.[31]

Perhaps this criticism of Gallie's account rests on an uncharitable reading. Often Gallie regards a tradition of thought as an exemplar. For example, when he discusses the concept of democracy, he writes: 'these uses claim the authority of an exemplar, i.e. of a long tradition (perhaps a number of historically independent but sufficiently similar traditions) of demands, aspirations, revolts and reforms of a common *anti-in*egalitarian character'.[32] Interpreted in this way, the requirement that an essentially contested concept be related to an exemplar would not appear to be vulnerable to the objection that

---

condition for sharing the same concept, I doubt that it is a necessary condition: if it were, many political concepts would be ambiguous – see pp. 82–3.

[28] Susan Hurley seems mistakenly to treat Gallie's attempt to distinguish confused terms from essentially contested concepts as an attempt to distinguish agreement from disagreement in forms of life (see *Natural Reasons*, p. 47). But that is not Gallie's aim: Gallie supposes that when people dispute the application of a confused term, they are not engaged in a substantive disagreement, but he does not think it thereby follows that they disagree in forms of life. Gallie allows the possibility that people might use the same terms to express different concepts but nevertheless share enough concepts for it to be true that they share forms of life and for communication between them to be possible.

[29] ECC, p. 180; PHU, p. 168.

[30] See, e.g. E. Gellner, 'The Concept of a Story', *Ratio*, vol. 19, 1967, pp. 49–66; J. Gray, 'On the Contestability of Social and Political Concepts', *Political Theory*, vol. 5, 1977, pp. 331–48; Miller, 'Linguistic Philosophy'.

[31] See Miller, 'Linguistic Philosophy', p. 42.

[32] ECC, p. 186; PHU, p. 180.

this is too restrictive, for a tradition can be understood simply as a pattern of judgements embedded in a practice; the existence of a tradition doesn't entail agreement on some actual historical case. But even if we did accept that a tradition could constitute an exemplar, Gallie's account would still be unsatisfactory because he gives us no answer to the crucial question of how we are to distinguish different traditions or to determine that independent traditions are 'sufficiently similar'.

Since Gallie, some of those who have subscribed to essential contestability theses, such as Steven Lukes, have tried to mark off disagreements over the application of essentially contested concepts from confused disputes over ambiguous terms by using a distinction between concept and conception, or some analogue of it.[33] In Lukes's view, when there is genuine disagreement, contestants must share a common core concept, even though they may have different interpretations of it: 'contests ... are after all, contests over something: essentially contested concepts must have some common core; otherwise, how could we justifiably claim that the contests were about the same concept?'[34] Unfortunately the claim that there must be a core common to different uses of political terms runs into difficulties when we try to give it a non-trivial interpretation and then apply it to actual cases of disagreement. If it merely amounts to the idea that if disputants are to be correctly said to be disagreeing over the proper application of a concept, they must share the same concept, then it would seem to be tautologous and trivially true. Suppose instead that we take it as Lukes seems to have intended, viz. as a proposal that a disagreement between contestants over how to apply a term correctly can be properly characterized as a dispute over the correct application of a shared concept if, and only if, there is some abstract definition which correctly captures their uses of that term. Then it seems that it cannot be applied in a straightforward way to distinguish disagreements over the application of shared concepts from disputes over ambiguous terms.

Although there are surely no grounds for denying that if people genuinely share definitions, they must share concepts, there can be problems with determining whether they really do share definitions. Agreement that some configuration of words provides a correct

---

[33] This technical distinction between concept and conception was first introduced by Rawls: see *A Theory of Justice*, pp. 5–6.
[34] Lukes, 'Relativism', p. 187.

definition of a term does not show conclusively that there is genuine agreement of a definition. Someone might agree that, for example, 'A exercises power over B' can be correctly analyzed as 'A affects B in a manner contrary to B's interests',[35] but argue that the word 'interests' has different meanings. They might then conclude that different uses of 'exercising power over' incorporate different concepts of interests, so 'exercising power over' is itself ambiguous. Such a claim may not be true in this case but the fact that it is intelligible and has some plausibility is sufficient to show that mere assent to a set of marks on paper or a string of sounds does not guarantee that there is agreement on a definition. Agreement that some configuration of words provides an adequate definition of a term does not incontrovertibly establish that this term has the same meaning for all its users; a configuration of words is no more self-interpreting than a Lockean idea.

Not only does the idea that sharing definitions is a necessary and sufficient condition for sharing concepts lack a straightforward application to distinguishing univocal from ambiguous terms, there is also the suspicion that it might mistakenly treat some terms as ambiguous because it is too restrictive. In *Philosophical Investigations*, Wittgenstein argues that there are no properties common to all and only those phenomena we quite properly call games, although 'game' is not an ambiguous term. We are justified in using the term 'game' to apply to many diverse activities because if we look at these activities 'we see a complicated network of similarities overlapping and criss-crossing: sometimes overall similarities, sometimes similarities of detail'.[36] If Wittgenstein is correct, there is no abstract definition of the term 'game'. Perhaps some key political concepts are of a similar kind, in which case it will be impossible to find abstract definitions of them which correctly capture their use; nevertheless it will not follow that they are ambiguous.

If sharing definitions were a *necessary* condition of sharing concepts, then it would appear to follow that different uses of a number of political terms would not be expressions of the same concept. For example, Christine Swanton argues convincingly that there is no acceptable abstract definition which could provide us with a

---

[35] This is how Lukes seems to define the concept of exercising power over: see Lukes, *Power*, p. 27; 'Relativism', p. 186.
[36] PI, section 66.

common core to different uses of the term 'distributive justice'.[37] She argues that the following principles constitute different concepts of distributive justice:

C_1: Whatever distribution of a social advantage arises from a just situation by just means is itself just.

C_2: A proper nonarbitrary balance between competing claims for a social advantage is determined.

C_3: There is a rendering of each unto his/her share or amount of social advantage.[38]

Swanton proposes that defenders of essential contestability theses should give up the idea that disputes over the use of terms such as 'distributive justice' are disputes over the proper application of a shared concept but not conclude that this means these disputes are confused. She suggests that it may be possible to defend the idea that they are genuine because they concern the correct characterization of the same 'thing'; 'the fact that terms lack a common meaning does not entail that they lack a common referent'. Her idea is that 'a theory of reference could be proposed in which rival theories are deemed to refer to the same thing by virtue of their agreement on sufficiently many "samples"'.[39]

Swanton's proposal, when taken as a response to someone who claims that those who disagree about how to apply terms such as 'distributive justice' fail to communicate, is problematic because it invites the challenge: how do we know that we are referring to the same thing? When there is widespread disagreement over 'samples', we are left unclear about how disputants *could be* referring to the same property. Swanton might just as well have suggested that we should give up the idea that sharing concepts requires that there be some abstract definition or 'core' common to different uses of a term, but should allow that agreement on sufficiently many judgements justifies the claim that they share concepts.[40] This would be vulnerable to any argument which could establish that sharing concepts requires more agreement in judgement than is available with political terms such as 'freedom' and 'distributive justice'. But it is not

---

[37] See Swanton, 'On the "Essential Contestedness" of Political Concepts', p. 817.

[38] *Ibid.*

[39] *Ibid.*, p. 818.

[40] Of course, this is vague: what constitutes 'agreement on sufficiently many judgements'? But perhaps this needn't trouble us: the question of whether disputants share the same concept may be one that cannot be settled by any precise method and may in some cases not have a determinate answer.

obvious that Swanton's proposal fares better for it is vulnerable to any argument which could establish that sameness of reference requires more agreement in judgement than actually occurs.

There are theories of reference available in the philosophy of language which, if true, would entitle us to say that scientists advocating competing physical theories which used the same term were nevertheless picking out the same kind despite significant disagreement over what counts as an instance of it. Causal theories of reference of a historical kind hold that the references of some terms are fixed by initial baptisms.[41] W. H. Newton-Smith suggests that 'the predicate ". . . is an electron" was introduced with the intention of picking out [the] kind of constituent of matter [that is] . . . causally responsible for the cathode ray phenomenon'.[42] So a theory which held that the reference of the term 'electron' is fixed by an initial baptism could claim that its reference is the same across different and conflicting physical theories that have been proposed since this initial baptism because in each of them it designates the cause of the illuminated patch sometimes seen on a cathode ray tube at the opposite end of the cathode. Alternatively a non-historical causal theory of reference might be proposed, according to which the reference of terms used in the natural sciences is fixed by the intentions of *current* experts to refer to the causes of phenomena, rather than the intentions of those who originally introduced these terms.[43] On causal theories, those who advocate different scientific hypotheses which, e.g. employ a term such as 'electron', pick out the same entities despite significant differences because they share an identifying description of the form 'A is the cause of B'. Can this approach help us to show that those who apply differently terms which (say) pick out *moral* properties, such as the expression 'distributive justice', are referring to the same properties?

Geoffrey Sayre-McCord points out that 'moral properties are traditionally thought of as firmly ensconced in the causal nexus: bad

---

[41] See, e.g. M. Devitt and K. Sterelny, *Language and Reality: An Introduction to the Philosophy of Language* (Oxford: Blackwell, 1987), ch. 5. Saul Kripke was the first to propose such a theory (see his *Naming and Necessity* (Cambridge, MA: Harvard University Press, 1980)) and his suggestion was developed by Hilary Putnam (see 'The Meaning of "Meaning"' in his *Collected Papers vol. II: Mind, Language and Reality* (Cambridge: Cambridge University Press, 1975)).

[42] Newton-Smith, *The Rationality of Science*, p. 173.

[43] *Ibid.*, ch. 7, section 6.

character has notorious effects (at least when backed by power), and fair social institutions evidently affect the happiness of those in society'.[44] If it is true that the reference of moral terms is fixed by naturalistic causal descriptions, then there is room for the argument that those who advocate different moral and political positions which use these terms are referring to the same properties because they are picking them out by the same descriptions of this kind. However, I do not think that we need to assume such a contentious account of the way in which the reference of moral terms is fixed in order to answer the person who proposes that political disagreement arises because the same term is used in different senses.[45] Swanton's chief insight is that a dispute can be genuine *even if* those involved in it do not attach the same meaning to the disputed term, i.e. do not use it to express the same concept. (That is something which, e.g. Gallie and Lukes failed to appreciate.) There may be something at issue between two people who disagree over the proper use of a term, even if it does not express the same concept for each of them; so disputants may be involved in a genuine disagreement when they contest the application of a term that has a different meaning for each of them. Therefore, even if key political terms were ambiguous, it would not follow without a lot more argument that the intractability of disputes over their application was due to a failure of communication. Let me explain this point further by considering some possible cases.

In *The Real World of Democracy*, C. B. Macpherson argues that our thinking about democracy is muddled because there is 'a genuine confusion as to what democracy is supposed to be about'.[46] He contends that 'democracy' is not simply a 'hooray' term, used merely to commend one's favoured social and political system, and distinguishes three different senses of it, locating them in different traditions: liberal, communist and Third World. In the first sense, democracy is seen as a system of government, based on competition between rival political parties – a way of choosing and authorizing

---

[44] Sayre-McCord, 'Moral Theory and Explanatory Impotence' in his *Essays on Moral Realism*, p. 265.

[45] Moral realists need not subscribe to this account of how the reference of moral terms is fixed: they may believe that it is fixed by moral descriptions, and hold that moral facts and properties are not identical with non-moral facts and properties even though they are constituted by them.

[46] C. B. Macpherson, *The Real World of Democracy* (Oxford: Oxford University Press, 1966), p. 1.

political decision makers; in the second sense, 'democracy' refers to a society in which everyone exercises their human powers and realizes their humanity; in the third sense, 'democracy' refers to a system of government in which the general will of the people is expressed through a single party. Macpherson addresses the issue of why all these different variants are called 'democracy' and he argues that they 'have one thing in common: their ultimate goal is the same – to provide the conditions for the full and free development of the essential characteristics of all members of the society'.[47] On this basis, it might be alleged that those who disagree over what counts as democratic are really involved in a genuine but difficult debate about what conditions provide for the full and free development of all members of society.

Suppose, however, someone were to argue that those who dispute the proper use of the term 'democracy' do so because they fail to understand each other, on the grounds that although the variants distinguished have one thing in common, different uses of 'democracy' nevertheless express different concepts.[48] That proposal could be defended only if reasons could be given for rejecting the following alternative view: that disputants successfully communicate despite employing different concepts because they are disagreeing over what conditions are required for the full and free development of all members of society, even if they do not describe their disagreement in these terms. This might be the case if they both thought that part of the point of the notion of democracy was to specify those conditions and each regarded the concept he was using as a successful attempt to do just that. One crucial test of the thesis that disputants disagree *because* they are employing different concepts of

---

[47] *Ibid.*, pp. 36–7.
[48] This claim would have some plausibility. After all, some conceptions of distributive justice have the same thing in common and justice is not the same as democracy. Initially Macpherson seems to present such a diagnosis of why people disagree over the proper use of the term 'democracy', e.g. he says: 'At bottom, the muddle about democracy is due to a genuine confusion as to what democracy is supposed to be about. For the word democracy has changed its meaning more than once, and in more than one direction ... Democracy has become an ambiguous thing, with different meanings – even apparently opposite meanings – for different peoples' (Macpherson, *The Real World of Democracy*, pp. 1–2). Later, however, he seems to suggest that disagreement is *really* about how to achieve the same ultimate end – conditions for the full development of each person's essentially human capacities. He writes: 'Differences in judgement about means commonly obscure the fact that [disputes] share the same ultimate moral end' (Macpherson, *The Real World of Democracy*, p. 37).

'democracy' would be whether they stopped disagreeing when they came to realize that they defined democracy differently. Under these conditions they might continue to disagree over the proper use of the term because for them this dispute was principally a disagreement over what conditions provide for the full and free development of each person's essential human capacities. (This needn't mean that the *reference* of the term 'democracy' is fixed by the description 'a system which provides for the full and free development of all members of society'; indeed 'democracy' has a narrower reference than that on both the liberal and 'Third World' uses distinguished by Macpherson. So I am saying something different from Swanton.)

Consider also the expression 'distributive justice'. Suppose Swanton is right that those who disagree over how to employ it do not share the same concept. What could be said in response to the claim that these contests merely result from a failure of communication caused by disputants mistakenly thinking that they shared a single underlying concept of justice? As David Miller has pointed out, those who disagree over the use of the term nevertheless concur in thinking that it refers to a manner of distributing goods among persons.[49] So the proposed explanation for the intractability of disputes over the use of 'distributive justice' would compete with more plausible explanations which maintained that although disputants didn't share the same concept of justice they were nevertheless communicating because they were involved in a genuine disagreement over how goods should be distributed amongst persons. That might be the case if each accepted that part of the point of the notion of justice was to specify the way in which goods should be distributed and each regarded his account as the best available attempt.

These considerations give us grounds for resisting attempts to exploit the (perhaps mistaken) idea that political terms are, in general, ambiguous in explaining the existence and persistence of political disputes. Even if terms were ambiguous, this would not show that those who use these terms with different senses disagree

---

[49] See Miller, 'Linguistic Philosophy', pp. 43–4. Miller seems to think that the fact that there is this much agreement is sufficient to show that disputants share concepts. I'm not sure that it is: suppose that someone argued that goods ought to be distributed according to eye colour – would this be a conception of justice?

over their proper use because they fail to communicate: they may nevertheless understand each other perfectly well.[50]

3 DISAGREEMENT AND INCOMMENSURABILITY

There is another version of the view that those who disagree over the application of political terms do so because they fail to understand each other which is more radical than those considered so far. This version, unlike those discussed in sections 1 and 2, denies the possibility of rational resolution to disputes over the application of political terms, and derives its inspiration from Thomas Kuhn's work in the philosophy of science. In *The Structure of Scientific Revolutions*, Kuhn developed an account of scientific change in which the advocates of competing scientific theories are conceived as presenting incommensurable paradigms. In this view, communication between rival theorists is at best partial and each has to learn to translate the other's theory into his own language. The idea that different scientific theories are embedded in incommensurable conceptual schemes has a natural analogue in the domain of morality and politics: advocates of different moral and political positions can be conceived as articulating theories that involve different conceptual schemes so that socialists, liberals and radical feminists (for instance) do not fully engage with each other when they argue over the proper interpretation of terms such as 'justice', 'democracy' and 'freedom'.[51] This might serve to account not only for the intractability of moral and political disputes but also for why these disputes, when they occur, are systematic and pervasive. It would constitute a version of the contestability conception of how political disagreement is to be explained.

Although highly innovative, Kuhn's original account contained a number of unclarities. He seemed to argue that a particular scientific term is defined by the theory in which it appears, and that when rival theorists use the same term in presenting their theories, it has a completely different meaning in each. For example, he wrote: 'the Copernicans who denied its traditional title "planet" to the sun

---

[50] I do not mean to deny that some disagreements over the proper use of political terms may rest upon confusion that is created by using the same term to express different concepts. In my 'Politics and the State' (*Political Studies*, vol. 38, 1990, pp. 575–87), I argue that disagreements over whether we should use the term 'politics' narrowly or broadly are often merely verbal.

[51] Cf. Lukes, 'Relativism'.

were not only learning what "planet" means or what the sun was. Instead, they were changing the meaning of "planet".'[52] Kuhn's use of the idea that the transition from one paradigm to another is analogous to a gestalt switch encouraged the view that he thought rival theorists completely fail to engage with each other and suffer from simple miscommunication. On this account, the switch from one paradigm to another must be an entirely non-rational process, like changing one's mind after a blow to the head with a blunt instrument. Debate may be essential in leading a person to change his or her mind, but its role can never be significantly different to that a blow to the head might play. In places Kuhn indeed seems to present such a picture: for example, he writes that anomalies and crises 'are terminated, not by deliberation and interpretation, but by a relatively sudden and unstructured event like the gestalt switch'.[53]

Kuhn apparently thought that theories could be incommensurable but nevertheless *contradict* each other. But if his account does hold that statements made from one theoretical perspective cannot be translated at all into statements made from the perspective of another theory, then it is impossible for different theories to contradict each other. On such a view, there could only be pragmatic grounds for choosing one theory in preference to another: so a particular theory might be chosen because 'there is no need for explanatory purposes to adopt both, and adopting both would have the consequence of pointlessly bloating our ontology',[54] but not because it provides a better explanation than its 'rivals' from some shared or neutral perspective.

An extension of this account into the sphere of morality and politics would lead to the hypothesis that those who apply moral and political terms differently suffer from simple miscommunication. It would have the implication that these disputes would not be settleable by coming to appreciate the reasons for preferring one application to another because different political theories (or ideologies) would be completely incommensurable. Since statements made from one political perspective would not be translatable into statements that could be made from another, they could not contradict each other. It would nevertheless be impractical to endorse more

[52] Kuhn, *The Structure of Scientific Revolutions*, p. 128.
[53] *Ibid.*, p. 122.
[54] Newton-Smith, *The Rationality of Science*, p. 159.

than one ideology since it would be impossible for a society to be organized according to the prescriptions made by different theories.

This view shares the Lockean idea that those who disagree over the application of political terms suffer from simple miscommunication but it does not seem to be vulnerable to Wittgenstein's implicit criticisms of the Lockean model of miscommunication. In addition, an incommensurability thesis of this sort applied to morality and politics might appear to be more defensible than one applied to the natural sciences. A standard realist objection to Kuhn's view maintains that a term in different theories may have the same reference even if it has a different meaning in each of them, and hence that different theories can be rationally compared. However, this objection to Kuhn's view is more effective when it is backed by a causal theory of reference (whether historical or non-historical) of the sort I described in the previous section; in the realm of ethics such a theory would seem to be committed to the view that the reference of moral terms is fixed by naturalistic causal descriptions (such as, for example, 'is conducive to the greatest happiness'), and many will find that idea unacceptable.

An incommensurability thesis is nevertheless highly implausible as an explanation of political disagreement in its contemporary forms because we do ordinarily think that we have at least some understanding of what our political adversaries are saying. We may be mistaken about *how much* we understand but surely it is outlandish to suppose that none of us have any understanding of political positions different from our own, or that we cannot comprehend political perspectives other than our own. Ultimately I think this phenomenological objection is sufficiently strong to defeat the view that different political ideologies employ entirely incommensurable conceptual schemes. I shall nevertheless develop a more theoretical objection; one which is inspired by Donald Davidson's writings.[55]

Consider two different perspectives on a political disagreement: the perspective of a person who is engaged in it, and the perspective of an observer. In the former case, if it really were true that someone had *no* understanding of what was being said, what grounds would he have for thinking that his opponents were saying anything

---

[55] See D. Davidson, 'On the Very Idea of a Conceptual Scheme' in his *Inquiries into Truth and Interpretation* (Oxford: Oxford University Press, 1984). (My conclusion is different from Davidson's since I don't argue for the claim that we can't make sense of the idea of untranslatable languages.)

meaningful at all? Why should he credit them with a different but incommensurable conceptual scheme, rather than treat them as wholly inarticulate? If he could observe a pattern in their noises, then he would be entitled to view them as genuine language users. But if he could observe such a pattern, he should be able to find some translation that was at least barely adequate. Someone might have the kind of deportment we associate with language use even if it were impossible to translate. But in this case, in so far as someone was persuaded that he was encountering genuine language use rather than mere noises, this would just give him reason to think that there was an adequate translation he hadn't yet found. Much the same problem emerges if we consider the perspective of an observer on the disagreement who is attempting to explain it. Suppose he could not understand what one (or both) of the disputants were saying. Why should he credit them with language use rather than the mere creation of sounds? On the other hand, if he could understand what both were saying (with or without translation), why should he think that they employed different conceptual schemes?

There is a possible rejoinder here. If someone were able to understand what was being said to him, he would nevertheless have reasons for thinking that his opponent (or the person whose language use he was observing) was employing a different and incommensurable conceptual scheme *if* he could justify the claim that in coming to represent what was being said he had to employ another conceptual scheme. But if the criterion for judging that two discourses are incommensurable is untranslatability, justifying such a claim would require giving grounds for thinking that two discourses really were untranslatable, and it is not obvious what such a justification would look like: presumably it would have to take the form of a felt inability to express adequately in one discourse the claims that are made in the other. The best prospect of giving sense to this idea seems to be *via* the notion of *partial* (as opposed to complete) translatability. The idea of a partial failure of translatability is not incoherent and indeed in some cases we may have good reason for thinking that it has occurred. Consider the process of learning a second language. To begin with we learn mainly by translating back into our mother tongue, but as we acquire a mastery of the new language, we stop doing so. Suppose after a number of years we came to think that there were shades of meaning in some second

92   EXPLAINING POLITICAL DISAGREEMENT

language that could not be fully captured in our native language –
and in this judgement agreed with other speakers who had reached
full mastery of both languages.[56] Surely this would give us grounds
for thinking that there were sentences that could not be fully
translated from one language to the other.

The strong incommensurability thesis which I began this section
by considering maintains that judgements made within one conceptual scheme are *completely* untranslatable into judgements made from
within another conceptual scheme. A weaker incommensurability
thesis of the sort just described is more plausible, however.[57] This
thesis, when extended to explain political disagreement, claims that
a political term used by a person who accepts one political ideology
has a meaning *partially* different to the meaning of that same term
used by someone who accepts a different ideology; this difference in
meaning, it is claimed, cannot be entirely compensated for by
translation. The meanings of terms are sufficiently similar that there
is some shared standpoint from which rational assessment is possible.
So rationality has a genuine role in political argument even though
it may be inconclusive. Political persuasion can come about by, and
in virtue of, the giving of reasons, but those who continue to disagree
about a political matter do so because they fail to understand fully
the considerations the other offers, and this residual failure of
communication is irremovable.

Is this an acceptable view? I think not. The issue is not simply
whether it is *intelligible* as an explanation of contemporary political
disagreement, but whether it provides the *best* explanation (or could
figure as part of the best explanation) of it. Like the view that there
is a complete failure of communication between those who disagree
substantially on political matters, it faces a phenomenological objection. When we reflect on political issues, we do not think that when
we take up one perspective on them, we cannot fully or adequately
represent other perspectives from the same standpoint. As Hurley
notes: '[we] find that examples of the sort provided by current
events and recent history – crimes of passion, mercy killings, acts of
political terrorism – or even the more bizarre cases found in science

See A. MacIntyre, *Whose Justice? Which Rationality?*, pp. 374–5.
Kuhn has subsequently indicated that this is the thesis he actually holds: see, e.g. section 5
of the postscript to the second edition of *The Structure of Scientific Revolutions* and 'Objectivity,
Value Judgement, and Theory Choice' in his *The Essential Tension* (Chicago, IL: University
of Chicago Press, 1977).

fiction stories, can be made sense of, and only rarely approach the horizon of unintelligibility'.[58] Of course, we may be mistaken in thinking that (without employing another conceptual scheme) we can fully understand those who defend very different political positions from our own; so the phenomenological objection is inconclusive and has only limited force. But it highlights a crucial disanalogy between the case of those who hold different political positions and the case of those who speak different and not wholly translatable languages: in the political case, there is no analogue of a person who has acquired full mastery of two different languages who, along with others who possess similar competences, senses that there is no fully satisfactory translation of sentences from one of these languages to the other. Therefore, we seem to have insufficient reason for making the claim that political disputes are intractable, pervasive and systematic because a person *cannot* fully understand the considerations given in favour of other positions. The fact that political disputes are extensive and persistent is compatible with the reality of communication between rival political positions. Postulating a partial failure of communication between them does not seem to help provide a better explanation of this fact in the face of the phenomenological objection, and taking into account the fact that in political discourse there is no analogue of the person who has full mastery of two different languages and judges that they are partially untranslatable. (None of this is to deny that there may be partial breakdowns in translatability between languages of political discourse. When, for example, we encounter cultures very different from our own, and try to make sense of their political ideas and practices from what is available to us, we may well be doomed to misrepresent and misunderstand them. Viewed in this light, some or all ancient political thought may be partially unavailable to us so long as we attempt to represent it in modern languages.)

4 ANOTHER KIND OF MISCOMMUNICATION

There is another conception available of what it is to misunderstand someone, which does not imply failure of translation or equivocation, but which permits us to say that political disagreement sometimes involves miscommunication. It requires us to focus on an

---

[58] Hurley, *Natural Reasons*, p. 51.

aspect of political disagreement already noted, viz. its interconnec-
tedness: disagreement over the application of one political term has
a tendency to precipitate disagreement over the application of a
range of other related terms. On what I shall call the ordinary
conception of miscommunication, one person fails to communicate
with another if she presents an argument with premises which the
other doesn't accept. The systematic nature of disagreements over
the application of political terms can often lead to this kind of
misunderstanding because someone will support a particular disputed use of a term by making a judgement that the person with
whom she is disagreeing turns out also not to accept; in this way
disputants 'talk past each other'. Alternatively someone will criticize a position in the belief that it is held by their opponent when in
fact it is not. Consider the following case. Some egalitarians,
properly so called, do not believe that equality of condition is
intrinsically valuable; they believe that it is instrumentally valuable
because in most circumstances the pursuit of equality through the
redistribution of resources provides the best means of benefiting the
worst-off group in society. For that reason, they are not vulnerable
to 'the levelling down objection' which is often pressed against
them, viz. the objection that they must believe that a society in
which everyone is in the same unpleasant condition is better in at
least one respect than a society in which a minority are in that
condition and the rest are more prosperous. To suppose that
egalitarians who view equality as a means to improving the circumstances of the worst-off are open to the levelling down objection is
to misunderstand their position.[59]

On the view I have in mind, the difficulty disputants encounter in
finding shared premises in order to start a genuine disagreement, i.e.
in reaching a position from which communication is possible, can be
regarded as a measure of how far they are apart. Miscommunication
needn't then be taken to show that there is no common ground
between disputants; nor does it imply that there are problems of
translation.

Consider cases that have been a concern of some of Bernard
Williams's writings within moral and political philosophy where
reasonable disagreement is both actual and possible – cases in which

---

[59] I owe my understanding of this point to Derek Parfit.

different values conflict.[60] One tolerably clear example is when honesty and openness conflict with a sensitivity towards another's feelings; when a person can't be honest, open and avoid hurting another's feelings. In situations such as these, a person seems to have a reason for being open (secretiveness is a bad thing), a reason for being honest (deception is a bad thing), and a reason for being dishonest (hurting someone's feelings is a bad thing). When people disagree over cases such as these – which are usually more complex and contextual than my brief characterization suggests – they may recognize that reasons exist for being open and honest and that a reason exists for not being so, yet disagree over which reason should be given most weight on balance. According to the ordinary notion of miscommunication, we have no reason to say that disputants in these cases miscommunicate. Each accepts that the consideration the other sees as decisive has some rational force, although they attach a different weight to it.[61]

In contrast, there are cases in which a person (or group of people) claims to perceive a conflict of values that others deny. On the ordinary conception of miscommunication, when someone sees a consideration as irrelevant for making a moral and/or political judgement that another thinks provides a reason for this judgement, then there may be a failure of communication between them. Something of this kind seems to exist between, for example, some radical feminists and some libertarians, when the former do not regard the fact that laws against pornography restrict acts of expression as a reason for opposing such legislation; the way in which pornography systematically degrades and humiliates women is seen by them as silencing this consideration, not as outweighing it. These feminists might be correct in thinking that a person who does not share their perspective does not fully appreciate the social meaning and significance of pornography. It might also be true that it would be impossible for them to bring him to share this perspective merely by argument. In that case his failure to appreciate the force or relevance of the considerations that were being emphasized would reveal a kind of misunderstanding or miscommunication.

The notion of miscommunication at work here might provide a

---

60 See B. Williams, *Problems of the Self* (Cambridge: Cambridge University Press, 1973) and his *Moral Luck*.
61 See also Kuhn's account of the choice between different scientific theories, especially in 'Objectivity, Value Judgement and Theory Choice', which I discussed in ch. 2, section 2.

small part of the explanation for the intractability of moral and political disputes but it would be of limited interest. It would take as a *premise* the fact that moral and political disagreements are systematic and pervasive, something which is just as much in need of explanation. So my survey of a number of different versions of the miscommunication thesis hasn't found one that is both true and does significant explanatory work. Even if key moral and political terms are used by different people to express different concepts, it does not follow that those who dispute their use are talking past each other. Hence not only does the miscommunication thesis fail but the basic idea behind essential contestedness theses remains intact; they would, however, be better expressed by saying that key moral and political *terms* are essentially contested, rather than by saying that key moral and political *concepts* are essentially contested, in order to avoid the objection that terms such as 'justice' and 'democracy' are used by different people to express different concepts. Essential contestedness theses, when they are clarified and qualified in the way I proposed in chapter 2, supply a promising general framework within which to construct explanations of why particular moral and political disagreements are so persistent: they recommend that we integrate rational and non-rational considerations in explaining why moral and political disputes are intractable. It is to this recommendation that I turn in the next chapter.

CHAPTER 4

Integrating rational and non-rational explanations

The qualified version of the thesis that key political concepts are essentially contested which I have defended involves an element that is part of the contestability conception of how moral and political disagreement is to be explained, viz. the idea that the proper interpretation of key political concepts is a matter of reasonable dispute. But this version of the thesis also includes a commitment to moral cognitivism, so it contains an element of the imperfection conception as well. Does it therefore need to give a central role to a theory of error of the kind envisaged by the imperfection conception?

Defenders of the imperfection conception have supposed that if a moral and political belief is mistaken, its incorrectness can be demonstrated to the satisfaction of every reasonable person who is fully competent in applying the laws of logic, and has the time and patience to think through the issues. In consequence the theories of error they have developed have included a proof (or alleged proof) of the incorrectness of the views which are held to be mistaken. But the account I have constructed does not need to give a theory of error of this kind a central role because, if my defence of the notion of an essentially contested concept succeeds, many beliefs may be incorrect (and be known to be incorrect) even though there is no argument that can be given against them which must satisfy any reasonable person with the necessary logical skills.

In this chapter I shall maintain that instead of developing a theory of error of some kind, we should seek empirical explanations which integrate rational and non-rational considerations in order to explain why moral and political disputes occur and persist. These empirical explanations are not intended to *replace* explanations which appeal to the kind of considerations discussed in chapter 2: the idea that consensus is not generally a primary aim of partici-

pants in moral and political discourse, that intellectual authority
has only a short reach within it, and the idea that key moral and
political concepts admit of different interpretations which are
reasonable, are intended to provide the general explanatory framework within which particular empirical explanations are developed.

In chapter 2, I distinguished between rational and non-rational
explanations for the holding of beliefs. Rational explanations appeal
solely to the reasons people have for their beliefs. In this context it is
also important to distinguish between an *objective* notion of what
constitutes a reason and a *subjective* notion: on the objective notion, a
consideration counts as a reason for a person to believe something if,
and only if, it is connected in the right way to the *available evidence*; on
the subjective notion, a consideration counts as a reason for a person
to believe something if, and only if, it is connected in the right way to
her *other beliefs*. On the objective notion, in so far as the same
evidence is available to two different people, what counts as a reason
for one person to believe something must also count as a reason for
the other to believe it. But that is not so on the subjective notion, for
according to it what counts as a reason for a person to draw some
conclusion depends on her actual beliefs.

On the objective notion, if a consideration is imperfectly connected to the evidence, it may nevertheless count as a reason for a
person to draw some conclusion; however, if the relation between
the consideration and the evidence is sufficiently weak it will be a
bad reason for her to draw it. Likewise on the subjective notion, if a
consideration is imperfectly connected to a person's other beliefs, it
may count as a reason for her to draw some conclusion but it will be
a bad reason if its relationship to her other beliefs is sufficiently
precarious. Both notions also allow that there are circumstances in
which a consideration would provide *no* reason at all for her to
believe anything, even when she thought it did: on the objective
notion this would be because it bore too weak a relation to the
evidence, whilst on the subjective notion it would be because it bore
too weak a relation to her other beliefs. In what follows I shall
employ the subjective notion of a reason, according to which a
consideration counts as a reason for a person to draw some conclusion only if it is connected in the right way to her other beliefs, but

shall interpret the phrase 'in the right way' broadly so that it includes bad as well as good reasons.

As I shall understand it, therefore, a rational explanation for why a person holds a belief explains by citing his subjective reasons for accepting it. Even if these reasons are bad, it may nevertheless be possible in principle and in practice to explain fully why he holds this belief by citing them. When a person claims as a reason for holding some belief a consideration that is wholly and obviously inconsistent with other beliefs that he continues to profess and act on, it does not count as a reason for him to hold that belief and can play no role in a rational explanation; a non-rational explanation is required. Rational explanations must make a person's acceptance of a belief *intelligible*. A person's acceptance of a belief may be unreasonable if she holds that belief for bad reasons, but nevertheless be intelligible; if she holds a belief which she has no reason to accept, and which flies in the face of other clearly incompatible beliefs, not only is her acceptance of it unreasonable, but her behaviour is likely to be unintelligible.

The idea that rational explanations must make a person's acceptance of a belief intelligible raises a question which I shall again refrain from attempting to answer, viz. whether reasons can be causes of beliefs in the very same sense that (for example) boiling water may cause a cold glass to crack. In my discussion of essential contestedness theses, I argued that some versions of them leave open the important possibility of providing explanations of political disagreement that *integrate* rational and non-rational factors: explanations which make reference not only to the reasons that people have for making the judgements they do but also to other facts, such as psychological propensities or personal experiences. Against this proposal it might be argued that rational and non-rational explanations are very different and cannot be combined. But even if reasons cannot be causes of beliefs in the same way that, say, personal experiences can be their causes, it would not follow that these different factors could not be integrated into a single explanation. The role of transformational experiences in belief formation could provide the non-rational part of the explanation for why a person came to regard some consideration as a reason for holding a belief, and then the explanation could be completed by relating this consideration to her new belief and her earlier beliefs, thereby providing the rational part of the explanation. A crude example: a person may come to believe that women should be allowed to decide for themselves whether or not to have abortions after he encounters someone who became pregnant as a result of rape. This experience may lead him to regard the idea that a foetus is a part of a woman's body as an important argument in favour of allowing women to make their own choices on this matter. (The consideration cited – that a foetus is part of a woman's body – may be in tension with his other beliefs if, for example, he believes that 'life begins at conception', but it nevertheless makes intelligible his pro-choice conclusion even if it provides a bad reason for it.)

A number of levels of explanation may be possible for why some belief is held, and particular explanations which are capable of operating at each of these levels are potentially very powerful. On the first level, a person's acceptance of a moral and political belief or theory might be accounted for in terms of a psychological propensity to be attracted to considerations which provide her with some rational support for that belief or theory, or in terms of a psychological propensity to find unattractive considerations that undermine it. On the second level, a person's psychological propensity to find these considerations attractive (or to find other considerations unattractive) might itself be explained in terms of various experiences that she has had, or various influences to which she has been subjected. On the third level, some account might be given of why that person was likely to have been subject to that set of influences or experiences, and to have developed the relevant psychological propensity, in terms of her membership of one or more social group (e.g. class, race, sex).

A pure version of the imperfection conception would also allow the possibility of explanations of belief formation at each of these levels of inquiry. Defenders of it might believe that the existence of a political dispute reveals that at least one of those involved in it does not have a clear understanding of the issues at stake (or, at least, is unclear about her opponent's position). They can allow that an individual's perceptions may be distorted by, say, her partiality, and that recognition may bring into play explanations at any of the three levels I have distinguished. Unlike a pure version of the imperfection conception, however, the conception I am defending does not give a central role to a theory of error in explaining why moral and political disputes are so extensive and persistent.

In some cases, a theory of logical error, i.e. a theory of why people commit logical errors when they reason, would undoubtedly have some role to play in accounting for why beliefs are held, but I suggest that its role in general would be less important than the imperfection conception standardly assumes. Jon Elster draws attention to one type of case where such a theory might have application. He suggests that there may be 'a natural cognitive tendency to believe that statements which are true from the point of view of any individual agent remain true when applied to the totality of all agents'[1] and employs that idea to give some fruitful reconstructions of Marx's theory of ideology. For example, he suggests that there is a tendency to infer from the fact that a worker is independent of any given employer to the conclusion that he is free from all employers, or to infer from the fact that any worker can become independent of capital as such that all workers can achieve such independence.[2] This example invokes what Elster, following social psychologists, calls a 'cold' mechanism of belief formation. Cold theories explain the acceptance of beliefs by reference to failures in cognition, whereas 'hot' theories explain it by reference to some motivational or affective drive. Hot theories, as well as cold theories, might generate part of a theory of logical error, for they might explain why various motivational or affective drives led people to make demonstrable mistakes in their reasoning about moral and political issues. In many cases of disagreement, however, when one party is mistaken the fact that they are mistaken cannot be demonstrated to the satisfaction of every reasonable person with full competence in applying the laws of logic, and the time and patience to do so, and they cannot be convicted of a logical error of this kind. What about the possibility then of a theory of error which did not assume that a person who holds false moral and political views has made a mistake in applying the laws of logic and allows that he may simply have judged incorrectly?

Theories of error, by their nature, provide non-rational explanations for why mistakes are made, i.e. they explain the occurrence of mistakes by appealing, at least in part, to non-rational causes. Elster argues that when non-rational causes are involved in the formation (or continued acceptance) of a belief, then there is a *prima facie* case for supposing that it is false.[3] Although in general non-rational

---

[1] Elster, *Making Sense of Marx*, p. 487.
[2] *Ibid.*, p. 211.
[3] *Ibid.*, p. 474.

causes tend to distort our thinking, in some cases they may lead us accidentally to the truth, so there is no guarantee that when they enter into the formation or continued acceptance of a belief that it will be false. The mechanism by which a belief is held is never sufficient to guarantee its falsity, hence I see no genuine prospect of distinguishing false beliefs from true beliefs on the basis of the mechanisms by which they are held. A corollary of this is that we can explain why a belief is held without making any judgement about its incorrectness; the falsity of a belief never plays a role in explaining why it is accepted. It follows that when a theory of error attempts to explain why someone holds a belief, its contention that this belief is mistaken cannot form a part of the explanation of why he holds it.

When a belief is true, the full explanation for why it is held will often involve the idea that it correctly describes the way things are: I believe that my dinner is burning because the smell reaches me, I see the smoke coming from the kitchen and I am reminded that I put the saucepan on half an hour ago. Here my belief that my dinner is burning is partly explained by the fact that it *is* burning. A partial explanation for the holding of this belief is nevertheless provided simply by my subjective reasons, constituted by the evidence supplied to me by my senses and memory; not much is left out of the explanation once these subjective reasons (and any non-rational causes) have been mentioned. Similarly if moral realism is correct, then the explanation for why someone holds a moral belief may involve the idea that it correctly describes the way things are from a moral point of view, but in general not much would be left out of this explanation if only the deliverances of her moral sensibility (together with any non-rational causes that are involved) were cited.

Consequently I propose that we can, in general, satisfactorily explain a person's acceptance of her beliefs by citing her reasons (in the subjective sense), and by making reference to any other factors (e.g. influences, experiences) that play a causal role in her holding them. Since the falsity of a belief does not play any role in explaining its acceptance, and the truth of a belief generally plays a negligible role, I think that there is much to be said in favour of remaining neutral on the question of whether moral and political beliefs which are likely to be controversial are true or false when the object is merely to explain their acceptance. In this way the explanation for why some moral and political belief is held does not incur any of the contentiousness of judgements about its truth or falsity. Since theories of error, even when they leave open the possibility of errors that are not due to mistakes in applying the laws of logic, must make contentious judgements about the truth or falsity of moral and political beliefs, we have reason to avoid them.

2 MATERIALIST VERSUS IDEALIST EXPLANATIONS

The distinction between rational and non-rational explanations is related to, although it is not identical with, a distinction that has been prominent in Marxist thought between materialist and idealist explanations. Non-rational explanations can be, but are not necessarily, materialist; all purely rational explanations are idealist.

Marx explained what was distinctive about his method by distinguishing it from 'idealism':

This conception of history thus relies on expounding the real process of production – starting from the material production of life itself – and comprehending the form of intercourse connected with this and created by this mode of production, i.e., civil society in its various stages, as the basis of all history; ... explaining how all the different theoretical products and forms of consciousness, religion, philosophy, morality, etc., etc., arise from it, and tracing the process of their formation from that basis; ... It has not, like the idealist theory of history, to look for a category in every period, but remains constantly on the real *ground* of history; it does not explain practice from the idea but explains the formation of ideas from material practice ...[4]

In Marx's view, what makes his approach materialist is the key role it gives to 'the mode of production' in explaining how forms of consciousness arise, i.e. Marx endorses a particular kind of non-rational explanation of belief formation. Like G. A. Cohen, we might distinguish between Marxist sociology – roughly, the claim that a person's consciousness is determined by his or her social being – and Marx's theory of history – an account of how one society transforms itself into another.[5] In the passage quoted, it is a sociological thesis that is being advanced, not a theory of historical change.

The explanations Alasdair MacIntyre offers in *After Virtue* for

[4] K. Marx and F. Engels, *The German Ideology* in *Complete Works*, vol. v (London: Lawrence and Wishart, 1976), p. 53.
[5] G. A. Cohen, *History, Labour and Freedom: Themes from Marx* (Oxford: Oxford University Press, 1988), pp. 176–8.

political disagreement in contemporary Western societies are, in Marx's terms, idealist. MacIntyre argues that competing positions in moral and political debate start from 'incommensurable premises' that 'have a wide variety of historical origins'.[6] These premises, and the concepts they involve, 'were originally at home in larger totalities of theory and practice in which they enjoyed a role and function supplied by the contexts of which they have now been deprived'.[7] MacIntyre speaks of 'practices', but for him practices are different from institutions,[8] and those he has in mind when he offers explanations of political disagreement seem to be moral evaluation and assessment: these practices are 'partially constitutive of the lives of social groups'[9] but do not include (though they may affect the organization of) productive activity, which in Marx's view, would have given MacIntyre's theory a materialist dimension. According to MacIntyre (in *After Virtue*, at least), those who disagree about moral and political matters in developed capitalist societies do so because they are the inheritors of a body of moral beliefs that is internally incoherent and which precludes the possibility of coming to agree through a rational process that is shared.[10]

I propose a less restrictive understanding of what constitutes a materialist explanation than the one that some Marxists have employed but which nevertheless distinguishes materialist explanations from the sort of explanations which MacIntyre defends: on the view I propose, an explanation is materialist if it allots power relations a key role in the explanation of how forms of consciousness arise. Arguably Marx uses the expression 'mode of production' to include the productive relations, which are power relations between people, labour power and productive forces in the process of pro-

[6] MacIntyre, *After Virtue*, p. 10.
[7] *Ibid.*
[8] For MacIntyre, institutions sustain practices, but differ from practices because they are concerned with 'external' rather than 'internal' goods: institutions are 'involved in acquiring money and other material goods; they are structured in terms of power and status, and they distribute money, power and status as rewards' (*After Virtue*, p. 181), whereas practices intrinsically involve goods that are 'realized in the course of trying to achieve those standards of excellence which are appropriate to, and partially constitutive of, that form of activity' (*ibid.*, p. 175).
[9] MacIntyre, *After Virtue*, p. 235.
[10] *Ibid.*, p. 49; p. 238. MacIntyre believes that there is no shared conception of rational inquiry which can be invoked to resolve disputes rationally. But he now supposes that one tradition of thought and practice – Thomism – can be demonstrated to be superior to others from the perspectives of each of the other traditions: see *Whose Justice? Which Rationality?*, ch. 18 and my introduction. I discuss these issues further in 'MacIntyre on Liberalism and its Critics'.

duction.[11] So when Marx says, for example, that a mode of production creates a particular form of consciousness, he also seems to imply that power relations play a key role in the construction of consciousness. However, Marx has a specific set of power relations in mind – those between people, labour power and productive forces: when he claims that 'it is not the consciousness of people that determines their being, but, on the contrary, their social being that determines their consciousness',[12] he means that a person's consciousness is determined by his or her economic roles,[13] and an economic role is constituted by a specific set of powers and constraints. I use 'materialism' to refer to a broader sociological thesis:[14] the idea that people's consciousness is conditioned by their social being, where social being (very roughly) is constituted by any set of social roles which significantly affect a person's opportunities in life. On this construal, gender roles, for example, are part of a person's social being.

In the next chapter I will offer a materialist account of *some* political disagreement which exploits theories about the way in which the sexual division of labour, which is founded on power relations between men and women, structures child-rearing practices in the bourgeois family and thereby constructs men and women differently so that they will find different moral and political ideologies and arguments attractive. This account does not deny the importance of institutions and practices other than the family and child rearing, but argues that those arrangements form us in crucial ways at an early stage. On the account I propose, personal transformations are possible, but there are systematic pressures in society that make them difficult to achieve. Although it has some empirical support, the account is partly speculative, and is intended to illustrate the possibility of explanations that are materialist and synthe-

---

[11] See R. Miller, *Analyzing Marx: Morality, Power and History* (Princeton, NJ: Princeton University Press, 1984), p. 205.

[12] K. Marx, Preface to *A Contribution to the Critique of Political Economy* (1859).

[13] See Cohen, *History, Labour and Freedom*, p. 45.

[14] The attempt to give 'materialist' a less restricted meaning has been a concern of some feminist thought: see, e.g. S. Harding, 'What is the Real Material Base of Patriarchy and Capital?' in L. Sargent (ed.) *Women and Revolution: A Discussion of the Unhappy Marriage of Marxism and Feminism* (Boston, MA: South End Press, 1981). See also Christine Delphy's work: 'A feminist interpretation of history is therefore "materialist" in the broad sense; that is, its premises lead it to consider intellectual production as the result of social relationships, and the latter as relationships of domination' (C. Delphy, *Close to Home: A Materialist Understanding of Women's Oppression* (London: Hutchinson, 1984), pp. 212–13).

size rational and non-rational explanations, rather than provide a well-confirmed model. (I draw upon theories which are controversial but try to defend them against the most important objections relevant to my project in the appendix.)

The account I develop maintains that the way we initially come to know the world is a function of our sex, but allows that it is also a function of, for example, our class and race in so far as these categories are important in our early experience. The account does not claim that gender is a more important factor in people's lives than, e.g. race and class, although it does involve the judgement that some sex-related differences in the way both adults and children perceive the world tend to hold across class and race, even though they may vary to some extent because aspects of child-rearing practices are specific to particular races and classes, or because of the class or race specific nature of later experiences.[15] Neither does the focus on child-rearing practices in the contemporary family prejudge questions that exercise, for example, radical feminists and Marxists concerning whether women's oppression is more or less important than class oppression and whether one can be understood and explained as functional to the other.

The account is coarse grained and, needless to say, individual lives are much more complex than it is able to capture. But it aims to point to tendencies and to suggest that we understand some patterns of individual difference as reactions against these tendencies. It is a piece of social science and as such cannot be biography. Although to have content it must be applicable to individuals, it illuminates only the broad outlines, rather than the details, of their lives. It leaves scope for more fine-grained understandings which focus attention on particular experiences and influences that in general are still structured by the institutions which it claims play a crucial role in moulding a general conception of the self in relationship to the social world.

3 THE SOCIOLOGY OF KNOWLEDGE

The approach to explaining political disagreement that I am defending lies within the sociology of knowledge because it recommends investigating the way in which social relationships influence

[15] I do not suppose that sex, class and race are *independent* variables: see part I, section 3 of the appendix.

thought, and proposes to construct this explanation in a purely 'empirical' way, i.e. without an evaluation of the beliefs it is attempting to explain.[16] But that tradition of research has often been treated with suspicion by political philosophers. Their mistrust of the sociology of knowledge has usually had one of three sources: firstly, a belief that it commits, or is liable to commit, 'the genetic fallacy'; secondly, that it fails to respect the participants' own view of why they hold the beliefs they do; thirdly, that it entails an objectionable relativism. Let me consider each of these worries in turn.

Consider the first idea. Logicians have named the view that one *refutes* a belief if one can explain its acceptance by reference to non-rational causes, 'the genetic fallacy': how a belief comes to be held is logically independent of the question of whether or not it is true. So coming to believe that some person's acceptance of a set of beliefs has non-rational causes doesn't *justify* a refusal to take his or her arguments seriously. Philosophers have insisted on a distinction between the explanation and justification of beliefs: identifying 'non-rational' causes of beliefs may serve to explain (partially or fully) why a belief is held, but cannot justify accepting or rejecting that belief. However, offering a non-rational explanation for the holding of some belief does not necessarily amount to committing the genetic fallacy for it may not implicitly or explicitly involve claiming (or thinking) that in offering this explanation one has refuted this belief. So whatever the actual and possible misuses of non-rational explanations of the holding of beliefs, it is still important, I think, to assess these explanations and to understand the proper role they can play in accounting for the existence and intractability of political disagreement.

The second worry about explaining a person's adherence to some moral and political belief in terms of non-rational causes is related to the first: if we offer explanations of this kind, musn't we fail to respect the holder of the belief's own view of why she accepts it? As a methodological principle, it seems correct to *start* from a person's own account of why she holds some belief if we are trying to explain her acceptance of it. But it would surely be mistaken to suppose that her own account will always be the full story, or even for that matter partially correct. We may not fully understand why we hold the

[16] See K. Mannheim, *Ideology and Utopia* (London: Routledge, 1991), ch. 5.

108   EXPLAINING POLITICAL DISAGREEMENT

beliefs that we do: we may be self-deceived or lack complete self-understanding. But don't we nevertheless fail to respect others when we refuse to take them at their word? I suspect that most of us have been infuriated by having our arguments discounted on the grounds that they are not the *real* explanation why we hold our beliefs. There are at least two different questions here, however: do we fail to respect a person if we don't take her arguments at face value?; if so, is that always immoral or inappropriate in some other way? Even if we were to answer the first question affirmatively, we surely should not answer the second question in the same way. In so far as we are interested in supplying *true* explanations, we should be concerned to uncover the real causes (whether rational or non-rational) for why people hold the beliefs they do and that may require us to override a person's own view of the matter. Of course, in conversation it may be rude, inappropriate, or simply unhelpful to assert that someone is unaware of the real explanation for why she holds her beliefs. But that is another issue.

The third worry about the sociology of knowledge has bedevilled it from its inception: is it committed to an objectionable form of relativism? The general problem here is one of how it is possible to accept what might be called 'historicism' without embracing a self-defeating relativism. Karl Mannheim, who is sometimes regarded as the founder of the sociology of knowledge, argued that it was committed to *relationism* but not relativism: 'relationism does not signify that there are no criteria of rightness or wrongness in a discussion. It does insist, however, that it lies in the nature of certain assertions that they cannot be formulated absolutely, but only in terms of the perspective of a given situation'.[17] Contemporary followers of Mannheim, such as Sondra Farganis, have also taken the view that the sociology of knowledge requires some kind of perspectivism:

The attitude of regarding knowledge or ideas as being related to one's social placement is itself explicable in terms of a post-Enlightenment questioning of, or even disillusionment with, notions of absolute reason or absolute truth, accessible to the individual in his or her ordinary existence or even to the social analyst using the canons of scientific inquiry . . . those who value a sociology of knowledge must raise, as part of their analysis, a critique of notions of objective truth or all-encompassing truth systems.[18]

[17] *Ibid.*, p. 254.
[18] S. Farganis, *The Social Reconstruction of the Feminine Character* (Totowa, NJ: Rowman and Littlefield, 1986), pp. 23–4.

It is not clear that relationism, as Mannheim describes it, is a stable position different from relativism. But in any case I do not see why the sociology of knowledge *entails* a critique of the notions of objective truth even if these notions deserve to be the subject of critical scrutiny, or even if some form of perspectivism is appropriate for epistemology: we should not confuse questions about the *justification* of a person's beliefs, or the question of whether it makes sense to say that a person's beliefs correctly describe some aspect of a reality that exists independently of them, with the issue of how we *explain* a person's acceptance of those beliefs.

Historicism is in my view plausible when it is understood simply as the claim that all thought is historically conditioned: that we cannot understand what is being argued, or why it is being argued, unless we investigate the social and historical context in which it occurs. Historicism becomes problematic, however, when it maintains that the proper standards of justification are completely determined by historical context, i.e. that what counts as a good reason for making some claim is fully determined by the existing practice. The conception I am defending does not take a stand on the issue of whether we can ultimately make sense of this form of historicism. For that reason I would prefer to say that this conception is part of the sociology of *thought* rather than the sociology of *knowledge*, for using the second expression tends to encourage the view that we must regard the question of whether some standard of justification is correct or appropriate as answerable only by historical investigation.[19]

19 Part of the problem here is that those working in the sociology of knowledge seem to understand 'knowledge' in an entirely different way from philosophers and from ordinary usage. See, for example, Tim Dant, who seems perfectly happy with the idea of there being 'false knowledge' (T. Dant, *Knowledge, Ideology and Discourse: A Sociological Perspective* (London: Routledge, 1991), p. 5), whereas philosophers would contend that this is a contradiction in terms.

CHAPTER 5

A model for explaining some moral and political differences

In this chapter, I shall try to show that psychological and socio-logical explanations of moral and political differences which integrate rational and non-rational considerations can be powerful, by developing a model that provides credible explanations of this kind for at least some moral and political disagreement. I begin by offering a characterization of some differences Carol Gilligan has claimed to discern between men and women's approaches to moral conflicts and show how, according to Gilligan, these approaches form parts of different developmental sequences which men and women progress through in their struggle towards moral maturity. Then in section 2 I present a theory of the construction of masculinity and femininity developed by Nancy Chodorow which, I propose in section 3, can explain the moral and political differences that Gilligan identifies. In section 3 I also attempt to show that the theory I develop has application not only to moral and political differences between men and women but also to differences amongst men and amongst women. Section 4 clarifies the explanatory model and exhibits some of its power by applying it to explain the acceptance of a particular conception of self-esteem – a sophisticated version of which can be found in the work of Robert Nozick.

I GILLIGAN'S THEORY OF MORAL DEVELOPMENT[1]

In her book *In a Different Voice*, Carol Gilligan attempts to articulate the difference between 'two ways of speaking about moral problems [and] two modes of describing the relationship between other and self'.[2] Her empirical studies associate these contrasting voices and

[1] This section is adapted from my 'Gilligan's Conception of Moral Maturity', *Journal for the Theory of Social Behaviour*, vol. 20, 1990, pp. 167–79.
[2] C. Gilligan, *In a Different Voice: Psychological Theory and Women's Development* (Cambridge, MA: Harvard University Press, 1982), p. 1.

modes of description with male and female perspectives on moral judgement and relationship. Gilligan's characterization of the differences between them can be captured, in its broadest outlines, by opposing answers to the questions: what is morality and why is it needed?; how do moral problems arise?; how do we resolve moral problems?

From the perspective that Gilligan finds present in many (but not all or only) men, which she calls an ethics of rights or justice, the need for morality arises from the fact that individuals have irreconcilably different goals and in pursuing these goals come into conflict: morality provides a set of rules to adjudicate. An ethics of rights supposes that people are *interdependent* in the following sense: if one person is to pursue his own goals without thwarting others in pursuit of their goals, there must be constraints on what one person can do to others. But it does not assume any stronger connections between persons: someone who reasons in accordance with an ethics of rights supposes that a person will in general be indifferent to others except in so far as they can affect his ability to achieve his own goals. According to an ethics of rights, it is a person's pursuit of his own goals which is of primary importance. From the perspective that can be associated with women, which Gilligan refers to as an ethics of care or responsibility, the necessity for morality arises from the interdependence of people. This perspective conceives of people as interdependent, not only in the way that an ethics of rights does, but also in the way that each person's life is embedded in a network of personal relationships which make moral demands; it is through the caring which is part of these relationships that individual lives are imbued with value and the social world coheres. According to an ethics of care, moral problems arise from conflicting responsibilities in relationships whereas according to an ethics of rights, they arise from clashes between competing rights or principles (where, we might say, these rights or principles standardly provide a means of resolving conflicts between persons). From the former perspective they are to be resolved by a contextual treatment that takes into account the needs of specific individuals, whereas from the latter perspective they are to be resolved by an application of abstract, impartial rules.

Gilligan's evidence supports the idea that men and women have a different set of moral priorities, or a different *focus of moral concern*, which is displayed in the different considerations to which they give priority.[3] It is this alleged difference I intend to exploit: a person who reasons according to an ethics of care is primarily concerned with meeting the needs of those to whom she is personally affiliated and with preserving her relationship to them, whereas a person who reasons according to an ethics of rights is primarily concerned with ensuring that conduct (especially the pursuit of impersonal goals) is regulated by fair and impartial rules. I shall also attach some weight to the fact that these perspectives give different accounts of why morality is needed: according to an ethics of rights morality is needed primarily because of the conflicts between different agents pursuing impersonal goals, whereas according to an ethics of care it is needed primarily because of the way in which a person's life is embedded in a network of relationships which each make demands.

Gilligan also claims that an ethics of care is contextual in a way that an ethics of rights is not. An ethics of care involves a sensitivity to the details of a situation. But that is not by itself sufficient to provide a point of contrast with an ethics of rights, for the application of an ethics of rights must involve some sort of ability to pick out the features of a situation in virtue of which the principles which constitute it are held to apply. If there is a difference between an ethics of care and an ethics of rights in terms of their context dependence, it must reside in one or both of the following two areas. Firstly, it might be held that an ethics of rights, but not an ethics of care is *codifiable*, i.e. that the content of an ethics of rights, but not of an ethics of care, can be specified in terms of an ordered list of principles or rights which determine what is morally required in any given situation.[4] Secondly, it might be held that an ethics of care does not even involve *prima facie* general moral principles because, unlike an ethics of rights, it does not assume that a feature which is morally relevant in one situation will be morally relevant in others.[5] In what follows I shall not presuppose that an ethics of care is contextual in either of these ways but if that were

---

[3] Cf. J. Grimshaw, *Feminist Philosophers: Women's Perspectives on Philosophical Traditions* (Brighton, Sussex: Wheatsheaf Books Ltd, 1986), p. 224. Some have claimed that Gilligan's evidence does not support any such conclusion. I consider these criticisms briefly in part II, section 1 of the appendix.

[4] Understood in this way, an ethics of care would resonate with the kind of virtue-centered theory that has been developed by those such as McDowell: see, e.g. his 'Virtue and Reason'.

[5] Dancy defends a form of particularism in 'Ethical Particularism and Morally Relevant Properties'.

so, it would provide a way of making sense of some of Gilligan's claims on this matter, which have often been dismissed by commentators.[6]

Gilligan's work also probes the way in which women's and men's moral reasoning evolves over time. It is concerned with the assessment of moral maturity and is a contribution to moral development theory. Gilligan identifies stages in moral development that transcend a pure ethics of care and a pure ethics of rights. In explaining how and why many women transcend a pure ethics of care, Gilligan appeals to mechanisms which include both rational and non-rational factors: the reflective processes that women go through and the crises that prompt them. She interviewed a group of women involved in abortion decisions; they were interviewed twice, once during pregnancy and once a year afterwards.[7] Her study suggests that some women transcend a pure ethics of care when confronted by moral conflicts in which there is no way of acting that avoids substantial hurt to others and themselves.[8] Gilligan claims that these crises often lead women to the recognition that their own needs should be taken into account in decisions. A policy of not harming others irrespective of the consequences to oneself can become self-defeating because in following it a person can cause such harm to herself that she becomes unable to help others or to meet their needs. Crises, such as those confronted in deciding whether to have an abortion, or to end a relationship, can lead women who are self-sacrificing to question the moral basis on which they act and to recognize the necessity of taking their own interests into account because the consequence of not doing so would have such tragic effects on their own lives that they would no longer be in a position to meet the needs of others.

Gilligan also seems to suggest that women who transcend a pure ethics of care as a result of confronting crises such as these come to have a greater *concern* for those to whom they are not personally affiliated (not merely an increased awareness of their rights to non-interference). She mentions George Eliot's idea that moral judgement will be lacking unless it is imbued with 'a wide fellow feeling with all that is human'[9] and maintains that:

[6] See, e.g. J. Grimshaw, *Feminist Philosophers*; W. Kymlicka, *Contemporary Political Philosophy: An Introduction* (Oxford: Oxford University Press, 1990), pp. 267–9.
[7] Gilligan, *In a Different Voice*, p. 108.
[8] *Ibid.*, p. 108; p. 118.
[9] *Ibid.*, p. 148.

when the concern with care extends from an injunction not to hurt others to an ideal of responsibility in *social* relationships, women begin to see their understanding of relationships as a source of moral strength.[10]

How is this transformation in the understanding of what it is to be a caring person achieved by women who face crises in which there is no way of acting that avoids substantial hurt to others and to themselves? Gilligan's idea seems to be that the recognition of the necessity of taking their own needs into account leads women who face these sort of crises to accept a principle of equality: they reason that their own needs have as much *right* to be taken into account as the needs of others, and that the needs of *all* others have a right to be considered, not just those of others with whom they are personally connected. In effect, the transformation of an ethics of care produces a commitment to a form of equality of consideration; a demand which also constitutes part of an ethics of rights.

Gilligan also has an account of how and why men often come to transcend an ethics of rights. She argues that a man's ethics of rights is transformed when he comes to appreciate what an ethics of care already understands, viz. the importance of attachment in human life and the moral significance of personal relationships. Gilligan thinks that Alex's way of conceptualizing moral problems reveals this kind of transformation:

Alex sees the need for morality to extend beyond considerations of fairness to concern with relationships: 'People have real emotional needs to be attached to something, and equality doesn't give you attachment. Equality fractures society and places on every person the burden of standing on his own two feet.'[11]

An ethics of rights transformed in this way converges to some extent with an ethics of care that has been transformed by a recognition of the moral need for equality of consideration: those men and women who reach these stages of moral development show greater agreement in moral judgement and greater similarity between their moral reasoning.[12] Gilligan seems to suggest that we can regard them as having a sense of self forged both in connection with and separation from others.

In *In a Different Voice*, Gilligan seems to argue that an ethics of

[10] *Ibid.*, p. 149, my emphasis.
[11] *Ibid.*, p. 166.
[12] *Ibid.*, p. 167.

care and an ethics of rights are largely complementary[13] even though they cannot be simply *conjoined*. She supposes that they can be *integrated* to at least some extent and are combined to some degree in morally mature people. More recently, on the basis of interviews she conducted Gilligan has argued that in morally mature people an ethics of care and an ethics of rights constitute two distinct 'orientations' which are not integrated, but which may be moved between in an analogous way to a gestalt switch.[14] However, it is an essential part of Gilligan's developmental model that a pure ethics of care is *transformed* by an appreciation of demands that constitute part of an ethics of rights, so she cannot simply abandon the idea of an integration of the two: a large part of her original research was concerned with the way in which a woman may come to recognize that an ethics of care is defective because it licenses the exclusion of her own needs in determining what should be done. (Gilligan also supposes that a pure ethics of rights is transformed by an appreciation of considerations that constitute part of an ethics of care, viz. the importance of attachment.)

Although Gilligan cannot simply abandon the idea that an ethics of rights and an ethics of care are integrated to some extent in morally mature people, there is nevertheless scope for that idea *and* the idea of a gestalt switch between the two perspectives to play a role in her theory: if an ethics of care and an ethics of rights cannot be *fully* integrated, there is room for the idea that a person might switch between the two perspectives in situations where the impossibility of full integration creates irreconcilable difference. To the extent that the integration can only be partial, different starting points may continue to affect basic moral orientations and lead to some divergences in moral thinking. In what follows I shall assume that, *in principle* at least, considerable (and perhaps complete) integration of an ethics of care and an ethics of rights is possible even if it is not realized in practice.[15] I shall refer to *the* integration of an ethics of rights and an ethics of care and shall assume that this achievement, which allows for some moral variations within it, is the ultimate stage of moral development. These assumptions are con-

---

[13] *Ibid.*, pp. 33 and 100.
[14] See C. Gilligan, 'Moral Orientation and Moral Development' in E. Kittay and D. Meyers (eds) *Women and Moral Theory* (Totowa, NJ: Rowman and Littlefield, 1987).
[15] Whether full integration of an ethics of care and an ethics of rights is possible in principle is a philosophical, not an empirical, matter. I see no grounds for thinking that the values they involve are radically opposed. Some reasons for believing this will emerge later on.

gruent with Gilligan's earlier work even if they are in tension with some of her more recent writings.

Gilligan's account of how and why men achieve at least a partial integration of an ethics of care with an ethics of rights again appeals to both rational and non-rational considerations. She argues that this transition can be a response to the experience of intimacy (which, Gilligan claims, many men rarely have) which leads them to see the deficiencies in an ethics 'abstracted from life', i.e. an ethics which lacks a genuine concern for relationship and connection:

> The experience of relationship brings an end to isolation, which otherwise hardens into indifference, an absence of active concern for others, though perhaps a willingness to respect their rights.[16]

Gilligan says nothing on the matter of how, if at all, men's attitudes towards those to whom they are not personally affiliated are affected by the integration of an ethics of care. But just as women's attitudes towards connections beyond the personal sphere are transformed by the integration of an ethics of rights, it is plausible to think that men's attitudes towards these sort of connections undergo a change when they come into contact with an ethics of care: a man's appreciation of the importance of genuinely caring about others in his personal life is, perhaps, coupled with a heightened concern for the lives of those to whom he is not personally affiliated.

It might be objected, however, that the need to form intimate, caring relationships within their personal life leads men only to a concern for family and friends. They might be willing to avoid illegitimately interfering in the lives of those to whom they are not personally connected but this does not amount to a concern for them. One plausible response is this: in so far as the need to care for those around him results in the formation of a coherent conception of how to live that is nevertheless based on an ethics of rights, his caring *cannot* be limited to his friends and family because of the principle of equality implicit in an ethics of rights: merely caring about individuals to whom he is personally connected would be arbitrary. What it is to care for a fellow citizen whom he doesn't know personally is, of course, different from what it is to care for a particular friend, but the principle of equality demands that he care for both.[17]

---

[16] Gilligan, *In a Different Voice*, p. 163.

[17] What caring in specific contexts and different relationships amounts to is discussed by Naomi Scheman in 'On Sympathy', *The Monist*, vol. 62, 1979, pp. 320–30; and by Grimshaw, *Feminist Philosophers*, pp. 215–24.

The principle of equality in this form does not always require impartiality; it requires the caring and emotional sensitivity appropriate to specific kinds of connection and, in personal relationships, requires the responses appropriate to specific friendships. In situations where impartiality is a moral requirement, e.g. in the treatment a person gives to others as a holder of a public office, to be impartial is to be *dis*interested, not to be *un*interested or unconcerned.[18]

Gilligan's studies also raise the issue of how those who, by whichever route, have reached the final stage of moral development distinguished above (in which an ethic of care is integrated with an ethic of rights) would understand the requirements of justice, and provision for those in need. Gilligan doesn't pay attention, however, to the fact that there are different conceptions of justice, different views about what rights, if any, there are, and different accounts of the relationship between justice and provision for the needy.[19] Her characterization of an ethics of rights is crucially vague in these respects. She writes that an 'ethic of justice proceeds from the premise of equality – that everyone should be treated the same'[20] and also that: 'For men, the moral imperative appears ... as an injunction to respect the rights of others and thus to protect from interference the rights to life and self-fulfillment.'[21] These characterizations are so vague that they can be read in such a way that they are neutral between, e.g. welfare-liberal and 'libertarian' conceptions of justice, where welfare-liberal accounts see justice as demanding that there be at least some provision for the satisfaction of everyone's basic needs, whereas libertarian accounts deny that this is a requirement of *justice*. However, Gilligan does talk of an ethics of rights as an ethics of *non-interference*,[22] which suggests that she thinks that the conception of justice implicit in a pure ethics of rights is a libertarian one: libertarian theories, such as Robert

---

[18] The confusion frequently made between 'being uninterested' and 'being disinterested' is, I think, significant here and functions to support a conception of justice based on non-interference.

[19] Cf. M. Friedman, 'Beyond Caring: The De-Moralization of Gender' in M. Hanen and K. Nielsen (eds) *Science, Morality and Feminist Theory, Canadian Journal of Philosophy*, suppl. vol. 13, 1987, p. 104.

[20] Gilligan, *In a Different Voice*, p. 174.

[21] *Ibid.*, p. 100.

[22] *Ibid.*, p. 100.

Nozick's, specify a framework within which people have the right to do as they please without interference from others.[23]

Gilligan does not explicitly entertain the possibility that the integration of a pure ethics of rights with an ethics of care might *transform* our conception of justice: the requirements of care for others might be integrated into it. She comes close to doing so when she says that an awareness of 'the multiple truths' supplied by an ethics of care and an ethics of rights 'leads to a relativizing of equality in the direction of equity and gives rise to an ethic of generosity and care'.[24] Previously she had characterized the concept of equity in terms of the recognition of differences in need,[25] which suggests that we might see integration of a pure ethics of rights and an ethics of care as transforming the conception of justice implicit in the former. Furthermore, as I mentioned earlier, she cites George Eliot's vision (or, more strictly, the vision of the narrator of *The Mill on the Floss*) that moral judgement should be informed by 'a wide, fellow feeling with all that is human'[26] approvingly as a vision of what an ethics of care integrated with an ethics of rights amounts to. As I argued, this suggests she thinks that someone who achieves such an integration comes to have a genuine concern for the interests of members of society to whom they are not personally affiliated. But if this is so, it is a serious question what form such a person's concern must take. (I say 'must' because the nature of what it is to have a genuine concern for the interests of others is a moral question not an empirical one.)

Several different conceptions of the relationship between justice and the care of those in need appear to be compatible with this integration. Most importantly, they include:

(1) a conception of justice on which it is a requirement of justice that people's needs be met and, perhaps, a requirement of justice that need alone should be the criterion for distributing some goods such as medical care. (Such a conception might not even be rights based.)

(2) a conception of justice, according to which it is not a requirement of

---

[23] See R. Nozick, *Anarchy, State, and Utopia* (Oxford: Blackwell, 1974). Of course, Nozick (and other libertarians) is not committed to denying that we may have moral obligations to help the needy; he may merely deny that these obligations are enforceable requirements of justice – see (2) on this page. Annette Baier overlooks the possibility of unenforceable obligations when she construes the concept of obligation as 'justified limitation of freedom' ('What Do women Want in a Moral Theory', *Nous*, vol. 19, 1985, p. 56).

[24] Gilligan, *In a Different Voice*, p. 166.

[25] *Ibid.*, p. 165.

[26] *Ibid.*, p. 148.

justice to provide for the needs of others, in conjunction with the claim that, nevertheless, it is morally obligatory (or, at least, morally praiseworthy) for individuals to provide help for the needy perhaps through private charities, although this obligation is not enforceable. (This conception is dominant amongst libertarians, so I shall refer to it as the libertarian moral and political perspective.)

(3) a conception of justice on which it is not a requirement of justice to provide for the needs of all members of society, conjoined with the claim that it is, however, an enforceable moral requirement that the needy be cared for, e.g. through the establishment of a welfare state which targets specific needs.

If the content of a pure ethics of rights were unaffected by its integration with an ethics of care, this would mean that the moral and political perspective which results from this integration would be libertarian (since an ethics of rights is conceived as an ethics of non-interference) and include the idea that although we may have moral obligations to help the needy, these are not enforceable (i.e. would conform to the perspective described in (2) above). But Gilligan has given us no reason for denying that the perspectives contained in (1) and (3) would result from the integration of an ethics of care and an ethics of rights. Indeed (1) and (3) seem to express more genuine concern for those who are incapable of taking care of themselves than (2) does.[27] To the extent that a network of private charitable organizations may leave gaps through which individuals slip because voluntary donations to different charities will be insufficient to provide for all those in need, or because individual charities deny them help on the grounds that the particular problems they face are not ones that the charity aims to deal with, it can be argued that a state-organized institution funded by, e.g. the forcible extraction of taxes, is more likely to provide proper care for those in need. An argument of this sort does not show conclusively that the libertarian perspective is incapable of demonstrating a genuine concern for those in need. There are moves that a defender of it might make in response. But irrespective of whether these moves could be successful, many theoretical and popular defences of the libertarian perspective make little or no attempt to show how a system of charities could be expected to ensure that

[27] See D. Miller, 'Altruism and the Welfare State' in J. D. Moon (ed) *Responsibility, Rights and Welfare* (Boulder, CO and London: Westview Press, 1988) for detailed arguments that different kinds of concern for others will make it rational for a person to support the welfare state.

everyone's basic needs are met, and to that extent fail to appreciate the moral demands of an ethics of care.[28]

2 CHODOROW'S THEORY OF GENDER CONSTRUCTION

Nancy Chodorow's account of the construction of gender[29] can, I suggest, explain some of Gilligan's findings and, therefore, can explain some of the disputes that result from the confrontation between an ethics of care and an ethics of rights and their transformed versions. Chodorow's account (as I interpret it) focuses on the nature of mothering in one of its specific historical and economic forms:[30] it offers an understanding of the construction of gender that applies to developed capitalist societies. These have three characteristics that are especially important from the point of view of Chodorow's theory: firstly, men have more status in these societies than women; secondly, men are absent from the home for most of the time in which children are awake; thirdly, it is only women who mother. Chodorow also regards the fact that only women mother as something that stands in need of explanation; her account does not assume that this is a 'natural' fact.[31]

Chodorow's account is psychoanalytic but makes significant revisions to Freud's. Let me outline Freud's own theory in order to

[28] The political vision that is implicit in Gilligan's conception of moral maturity is not confined to a position on justice and state provision of care for the needy. It is plausible to maintain that the integration of an ethics of care with an ethics of rights would also generate different commitments to community and citizenship: different conceptions of what citizenship and democracy consist in, and a different understanding of what is valuable about them.

[29] See N. Chodorow, *The Reproduction of Mothering: Psychoanalysis and the Sociology of Gender* (Berkeley and LA, CA: University of California Press, 1978); *Feminism and Psychoanalytic Theory* (Cambridge: Polity, 1989), especially introduction, chs 2, 3 and 5.

[30] Perhaps this was not the way in which Chodorow originally intended her theory, but she would now concede that it is the right way to read it: see *Feminism and Psychoanalytic Theory*, p. 15. I shall not always make a point of noting where the account I am advancing may differ from Chodorow's as she presents it in *The Reproduction of Mothering*. In order to avoid cluttering the exposition, I have not considered objections to Chodorow's account in this chapter; I deal with the most relevant of them in part 1 of the appendix.

[31] As a generalization about our society (and, as far as I know, all documented societies) it is true that only women mother. But the universality of this phenomenon should not make us think that it is a necessary feature of the organization of social life. It is a fact that only women can bear children, but there is no evidence to suggest that men are incapable of raising children and providing them with the kind of nurturing that is necessary for them to grow into 'well-adjusted' adults. (Chodorow argues that men acquire the basic capacities required if they have a satisfactory early relationship with their mothers: see N. Chodorow, *The Reproduction of Mothering*, ch. 5.)

bring out their differences.[32] Freud claimed that infants have a sexuality which goes through three over-lapping stages: oral, anal and phallic. The first object of a boy's sexuality after he enters the phallic stage comes to be his mother; that person who has cared for him and nurtured him throughout his early months. But he has a rival for his mother, his father, who imposes a strict prohibition on his desires. The boy comes to fear castration by his father as a punishment for his feelings towards his mother[33] and, as a result, the boy resolves his 'Oedipus complex' by repressing the desire for his mother into his unconscious, and identifying with his father; identification with his father promises the fruits of the masculine world as well as an end to his fear of castration. This resolution includes the fashioning of a super-ego out of the ego; the super-ego can be thought of as a set of internalized commands and prohibitions.

The first person to be an object of a girl's sexuality is also her mother. On Freud's account of the development of masculinity, it is the boy's Oedipus complex (his desire for his mother) which results in his castration complex (his fear of castration by his father). But on Freud's account of the construction of femininity, the relationship is reversed. Girls have a sense of inferiority because of their lack of a penis, and develop penis envy. They blame their mothers for their lack of penises[34] and turn to their fathers in the hope that he can give them one. Then, through a symbolic equation of 'penis' and 'baby', they come to desire a baby from their fathers. So on Freud's account of the construction of femininity, it is the girl's castration complex (her sense that she is castrated) which results in her Oedipus complex (her desire for a baby from her father, through sexual union with him).[35]

For the girl, the Oedipus complex does not require resolution

---

[32] The account I proceed to offer is a distillation of Freud's views as they evolve in 'Three Essays on the Theory of Sexuality' in *The Standard Edition of the Complete Works of Sigmund Freud* (trans and ed) J. Strachey (London: Hogarth Press, 1955) (hereafter referred to as SE), vol. VII, 'The Ego and the Id', 'The Infantile Genital Organization: An Interpolation into the Theory of Sexuality', 'The Dissolution of the Oedipus Complex', 'Some Psychical Consequences of the Anatomical Distinction between the Sexes' in SE vol. XIX, and 'New Introductory Lectures on Psychoanalysis', lecture 33, SE vol. XXII.

[33] On Freud's account, this fear generally has two sources. First, an explicit threat of castration often made by the mother, uttered in order to curtail the boy's masturbatory activity, with the warning that it will be carried out by the father. Secondly, the boy notices the anatomical differences between himself and girls; he regards girls as castrated, and so entertains the possibility that he too could come to lose his much-valued appendage.

[34] See SE vol. XIX, p. 254.

[35] *Ibid.*, p. 256.

through a massive act of repression in the way that it does for the boy under the perceived threat of castration. Indeed, Freud suggests that girls do not resolve their Oedipus complex, but rather allow the desire that causes it to dissipate slowly: 'One has the impression that [the girl's] Oedipus complex is ... gradually given up because [the wish to have a baby by her father] is never fulfilled.'[36] Later, he wrote that the Oedipus complex 'may be slowly abandoned or dealt with by repression, or its effects may persist far into women's mental life'.[37] The primary outcome of the girl's Oedipus complex is the development of a heterosexual orientation: the girl cannot bear her father's child, so she seeks out another man to give her a baby.

This completes my schematic account of Freud's theory of psychosexual development. Against Freud, Chodorow argues that gender is acquired by both sexes by the time a child is three, i.e. gender is established (at least in part) during what is, on Freud's account, the pre-Oedipal phase;[38] it cannot be, as Freud thought it was, mainly a result of the Oedipus complex. Although Freud acknowledged in passing[39] that the pre-Oedipal phase is different for girls than for boys, he attached no theoretical weight to this difference when he came to offer his account of gender development. Chodorow, in contrast, makes the pre-Oedipal phase central to her account. She argues that the pre-Oedipal phase is not only longer for girls, but also of a different nature.

The pre-Oedipal phase for both sexes is when a sense of self is acquired. The newborn infant does not distinguish itself from its primary caretaker – its mother – nor from the rest of the world in general.[40] During its early months, it begins to distinguish itself and in doing so develops a rudimentary sense of self. Chodorow claims that this process continues into the girl's fourth or fifth year, whereas for a boy it is, in general, passed through by his third year.[41] At the end of the boy's pre-Oedipal phase, his relation to his mother becomes embedded in a triangular conflict for he comes to perceive his father as a rival for her. In contrast, Chodorow argues, a girl

---

[36] *Ibid.*, p. 179.

[37] *Ibid.*, p. 257.

[38] See Chodorow, *The Reproduction of Mothering*, p. 150 and footnote 46, p. 230 for references. She relies heavily on Stoller's work: see R. J. Stoller, *Sex and Gender: On the Development of Masculinity and Femininity* (London: Hogarth Press, 1968).

[39] See SE vol. XXII, p. 119.

[40] Chodorow uses the term 'mother' synonymously with 'primary caretaker', rather than synonymously with 'female parent', and I follow her in doing so.

[41] See Chodorow, *The Reproduction of Mothering*, p. 96.

remains in a 'two person attachment' to her mother for longer and is not preoccupied with her father until later:

The content of a girl's attachment to her mother differs from a boy's precisely in that it is not at this time Oedipal (sexualized, focused on possession, which means focused on something clearly different and opposite).[42]

Chodorow suggests tentatively that the different lengths of the pre-Oedipal phase for boys and girls, and its different nature for the two sexes, can be explained in terms of the different ways in which mothers experience boys and girls and, consequently, the different ways in which they treat them.[43] Because mothering is almost always done by women, mothers experience and treat daughters as continuous with themselves, whereas they experience and treat sons as different from themselves:

Because they are the same gender as their daughters, and have been girls, mothers of daughters tend not to experience these infant daughters as separate from them in the same way as do mothers of infant sons. In both cases, a mother is likely to experience a sense of oneness and continuity *vis-à-vis* daughters.[44]

Mothers tend to treat daughters as if they had desires and needs the same as or analogous to their own, or as if their daughters had the desires and needs they ought to have rather than those they actually have. In contrast mothers tend to treat sons as sexual others, with needs and desires different from their own.

This asymmetry in maternal care means that girls and boys experience their mothers differently. Boys experience mothers as distinct beings before girls do and, because they are treated as 'others' (i.e. as different, not merely distinct), they develop and

---

[42] *Ibid.*, p. 97.

[43] Here she has in mind phenomena such as 'nuance, tone, quality' (Chodorow, *The Reproduction of Mothering*, p. 99). Evidence of differential treatment of boys and girls at an early age is difficult to assess (see S. Weitz, *Sex Roles: Biological, Psychological and Social Foundations* (New York: Oxford University Press, 1977), pp. 64–5), but does not refute Chodorow's suggestion. Stoller, whom Chodorow relies upon for evidence for the claim that gender is acquired by both sexes by age three, argues that (for both sexes) core gender identity is usually a result of three forces: anatomy, socialization and biology: 'core gender identity is produced in the normal by the anatomy and physiology of the genitalia, by attitudes of parents, siblings and peers and by a biological force' (Stoller, *Sex and Gender*, p. 47). Chodorow doesn't seem to accept a biological component; Stoller thinks that the biological component, although present, is less significant than the other two (see, e.g. Chodorow, *The Reproduction of Mothering*, p. 23).

[44] Chodorow, *The Reproduction of Mothering*, p. 109.

internalize a sense of self in terms of *separation*. In contrast, girls experience their mothers as continuous with themselves and when they develop a sense of self as distinct from their mothers, it is in terms of sameness; they see themselves as *connected* to their primary caretakers. Boys and girls also acquire different rudimentary gender identities:[45] boys acquire a sense of themselves as fitting into a general category *different* from their primary caretakers, whereas girls acquire a sense of themselves as fitting into a general category the *same* as their primary caretakers.

According to Freud, during the Oedipal phase the boy acquires his masculine roles by identification with his father and represses his love for his mother under the perceived threat of castration. However, Chodorow points to evidence which suggests that the presence of the father is not vital for the boy's acquisition of masculine roles (nor for his full gender identity). Normally in capitalist societies, fathers are absent from the family for most of the hours during which children are awake and so children receive little contact with them; furthermore, when fathers are absent all the time, boys do not apparently experience any more difficulty in acquiring masculine roles. A psychoanalytic account can accommodate these facts: it can maintain that boys are moved to acquire their masculine roles largely because they become aware of the status of men in society which makes masculinity appear attractive – and being masculine involves repressing his love for his mother. The boy acquires masculine roles not primarily by identifying with his father, but mainly by a precarious denial of all that is feminine, as represented by his mother (and also sometimes by identifying with cultural stereotypes of masculinity or men chosen as masculine models).[46] This has the important added implication that boys learn their masculine roles primarily by a *denial of connectedness*.

On Freud's theory, the girl's Oedipal phase is when she acquires her heterosexual orientation, and some of her (other) feminine roles. Chodorow's explanation for these processes differs from Freud's. Although it continues to give importance to the idea of penis envy,

---

[45] I understand a gender identity to be a sense of oneself as fitting into one of two exclusive social categories: the masculine and the feminine (see Scheman, 'Individualism and the Objects of Psychology' in S. Harding and M. Hintikka (eds) *Discovering Reality: Feminist Perspectives on Epistemology, Metaphysics, Methodology and the Philosophy of Science* (Dordrecht, Holland: Reidel, 1983), p. 236). As such, and because it is deeply rooted, I take gender identity to be a part of a person's sense of self.

[46] Chodorow, *The Reproduction of Mothering*, p. 176.

that idea is fundamentally re-interpreted. It no longer assumes that the penis is intrinsically superior to female genitalia, nor that it is perceived to be so. Instead the girl's envy of the penis is regarded as a response to the social meaning of having a penis in a patriarchal society: the penis symbolizes independence from the mother and the social privileges of men.

In Chodorow's view, the girl's acquisition of heterosexuality is to be explained, at least partially, as follows. Firstly, when fathers are present, they behave in a seductive manner towards their daughters (and men, in general, behave in this way to little girls) and encourage them to flirt.[47] Chodorow reports that complete and permanent father absence does not correlate with homosexuality in women,[48] but also appeals to evidence that adolescent girls from father-absent homes are uncomfortable and insecure with men and boys.[49] This suggests, perhaps, that although girls from father-absent homes may acquire an erotic heterosexual orientation because, for example, of social pressures and the devaluation of women, they do not fully learn what is culturally regarded as appropriate heterosexual behaviour. Secondly, girls experience a kind of rejection from their mothers: they begin to realize that their mothers value maleness more than femaleness and, indeed, that women in general are considered to be less valuable than men and are given less status than them:

What a girl comes to realize is that her common genital arrangement with her mother does not work to her advantage in forming a bond with her mother, does not make her mother love her more. Instead, she finds out her mother *prefers* people like her father (and brother) who have penises.[50]

Thirdly, the difference between the pre-Oedipal phase for boys and that for girls has an important consequence for the girl's Oedipal phase which may partially account for her turn to her father. During the Oedipal phase, girls are still concerned with issues involving individuation because mothers treat girls as continuous with themselves. *One* means a girl has for at least partially resolving this preoccupation is to turn to her father whom she can experience as an other and so develop a sense of herself as distinct from her primary caretaker:

[47] *Ibid.*, p. 118.
[48] *Ibid.*, p. 175.
[49] *Ibid.*, p. 138.
[50] *Ibid.*, p. 125.

A girl is likely to turn to [her father], regardless of his gender or sexual orientation, as the most available person who can help her to get away from her mother. The turn to the father then, whatever its sexual meaning, also concerns emotional issues of self and other.[51]

In situations where the father is permanently absent, then the second mechanism by which the girl acquires her heterosexuality (she feels rejected by her mother) may still operate. Analogues of the first and third mechanisms may also still function, since adult men with whom the girl comes into contact may flirt with her and a 'turn' towards them may provide her with a means of individuating herself from her mother.

Chodorow argues that daughters do not *reject* their mothers if they have fathers to whom they can 'turn', but add their attachments to their fathers on to their emotional bonds with their mothers. She argues that although there is a measure of hostility and rivalry between mother and daughter, this is never so great as the hostility and rivalry the son experiences in relation to his father prior to the resolution of his Oedipus complex, and that the daughter's attachment to her father is best understood as an addition to, rather than a replacement for, the daughter's earlier attachment to her mother:

A girl develops important Oedipal attachments to her mother as well as to her father. These attachments, and the way they are internalized, are built upon, and do not replace, her intense and exclusive pre-Oedipal attachment to her mother and its internalized counterpart.[52]

So the Oedipal triangle, when it exists, has a greater relational complexity for girls than for boys since it involves two strong attachments, rather than one.

Girls repress their Oedipal love for their fathers (if they can and do turn to them) but the psychological consequences of this act are very different from the consequences of the boy's repression of his love for his mother. This is because the girl's Oedipal attachment to her father is not so strong as the earlier formed bond a boy (and, indeed, a girl) has with the mother:

the organization of parenting generates a relational situation in a girl's Oedipus complex in which she does not need to repress her Oedipal attachments so thoroughly as a boy does. Her attachment to her father in particular is idealized and less intense than a boy's to his mother.[53]

[51] *Ibid.*, p. 121.
[52] *Ibid.*, p. 127.
[53] *Ibid.*, p. 133.

Girls learn most of their feminine roles by identification with their mothers, in a context of relationship, so their full gender identity, like their rudimentary one, is constructed in terms of sameness; they do not learn their gender roles in the way that boys generally do, by a denial of connection.[54] Girls may also learn some of their gender roles by instruction from their fathers and other men, particularly those bound up with heterosexuality such as flirting behaviour. But even then, these roles are learnt in a context of relationship, although they do not involve identification with another.

For my purposes, the most important part of Chodorow's account is her idea that men tend to develop a sense of self in terms of separation, women a sense of self in terms of connection, and her theory of how this comes about. A person with a sense of self in terms of connection will tend to define herself in terms of her personal relationships (e.g. I am x's wife, daughter, girlfriend) and by activities which bring her into affiliation with others; she will also attach much value to these attachments, and to activities that enrich and strengthen her relationships. A person with a sense of self in terms of separation, in contrast, will usually define herself in terms of goal-focused activities, character traits, physical characteristics and the like; she will also value these features of herself and her life considerably.[55] Note that a person may have a sense of self in terms of separation *and* connection, since she may (for example) define herself in terms of her goals *and* in terms of her personal relationships, and attach considerable value to both. How people conceive of their relationship, or lack of it, to others is given by the way they respond to experiences such as intimacy and isolation,[56] dependence and independence and their responses to

---

54 It is also compatible with this account to hold that girls may learn some of their gender roles from other models, such as teachers at school or friends. They would still be learnt in the context of relationship.

55 A sense of self does not necessarily fall into one of these two types. A person might have a sense of self in terms of membership of some ethnic group, or in terms of their nationality, which would not count either as a sense of self in terms of connection (since relationships to others in the same ethnic group or nation are not generally personal), nor separation. However, a person who has a sense of self in terms of belonging to some group may also have a sense of self in terms of separation or connection depending on other facts about them.

56 See Gilligan and Pollack's study in which four pictures – two showing a man and a woman in 'close personal affiliation' and another two showing people in 'impersonal achievement situations' – were presented to a set of male and female subjects who were asked to write stories based on them. Gilligan argues plausibly that the best explanation

the experience of others. Both linguistic and non-linguistic behaviour can be relevant in assessing their reactions.

Chodorow claims that those who possess a sense of self in terms of connection (unlike those who possess a sense of self in terms of separation only) tend to experience another's needs and feelings as their own[57] and experience themselves as continuous with others.[58] She is not always clear how she understands these expressions[59] but I think what she means is that those who possess a sense of self in terms of connection tend to have a well-developed capacity for imaginative understanding (or at least, have the psychological constitution necessary for such a capacity) and represent vividly to themselves the needs and desires of others. To these ideas we can add another of Chodorow's themes: that those who possess a sense of self in terms of connection will, in general, be amenable to changing their own preferences, desires and goals to permit others close to them to fulfil their projects. (They may simply subordinate their own projects to the projects of those around them, or, indeed, never develop any goals of their own, but this isn't an essential part of what it is to have such a psychology.)

Other forms of socialization and role training apart from those that Chodorow identifies, and which are often (also) coercive in character, undoubtedly play an important role in the acquisition of masculinity and femininity. Psychoanalytic accounts need not deny this, even though they do deny that they are the only important factors. Furthermore, the different senses of self that girls and boys acquire and internalize as a result of their early relationships with their parent(s) *tend* to be reinforced in later life by the sexual division of labour that exists in both the family and the market. Within the family, women bear primary responsibility for the nurturing that is required in order to raise children and they also, in general, provide their husbands (or male lovers) with the caring that sustains them emotionally. The sexual division of labour within the family is mirrored, to a large extent, by a sexual division of labour in the

---

for why those men who projected violence into the pictures of affiliation did so, is that they have a sense of self in terms of separation, whereas the best explanation for why those women who projected violence into pictures of impersonal achievement did so, is that they have a sense of self in terms of connection (see Gilligan, *In a Different Voice*, pp. 40–4).

[57] See Chodorow, *The Reproduction of Mothering*, p. 167.

[58] *Ibid.*, p. 169.

[59] See Grimshaw, *Feminist Philosophers*, pp. 180–1.

market;[60] the caring and nurturing that women give their husbands and children is mirrored, for example, by the caring and nurturing women as secretaries give their bosses, and women as nurses give their patients – and the housework and preparation of food women do at home is mirrored by the service work they do in the market. As a generalization that has exceptions, we might say that to the extent jobs in the market involve the exercise of nurturing skills, they are performed by women.[61]

The last century has seen a gradual increase in the percentage of women who work in the market,[62] but there is little evidence to suggest that the work women have traditionally done within the family – including child-rearing and nurturing – is being done by others.[63] So a large proportion of women's lives is still spent engaging in nurturing activities, thereby developing their nurturing skills, even if many women who work in the market do not perform jobs that involve the exercise of these skills. The tendency of the sexual division of labour that exists within the family and the market is to develop women's relational capacities, even if other features of the division of labour and the market tend to stunt the growth of these capacities. In contrast, the lives men lead in the family and the jobs they perform in the market don't, in general, require the exercise of nurturing skills, and in consequence they don't develop whatever relational capacities they possess. Hence, for men and women work in general will tend to reinforce the senses of self constructed during infancy, rather than change them.

3 THE EXPLANATORY MODEL SKETCHED

Gilligan's claim that men tend to reason according to an ethics of rights whereas women tend to reason according to an ethics of care can, I propose, be satisfactorily explained by Chodorow's theory of

---

[60] See H. Hartmann, 'The Unhappy Marriage of Marxism and Feminism: Towards a More Progressive Union', p. 25, and A. Ferguson and N. Folbre, 'The Unhappy Marriage of Patriarchy and Capitalism', p. 319, both in L. Sargent (ed) *Women and Revolution: A Discussion of the Unhappy Marriage of Marxism and Feminism* (Boston, MA: South End Press, 1981).

[61] Although it is true that most women who work in the market perform service jobs, such as cleaning and catering, which do not require the exercise of nurturing skills.

[62] See A. Ferguson and N. Folbre, 'The Unhappy Marriage of Patriarchy and Capitalism', p. 325, for figures concerning the increasing proportion of women working in the market in the US.

[63] Chodorow, *The Reproduction of Mothering*, p. 27.

gender construction. Briefly: an ethics of care, with its focus on personal relationships – conceived as the primary source of value in people's lives – can be found in women's reasoning because they tend to develop a sense of self in terms of connection only, as a result of child-rearing practices and the relative status of men and women in developed capitalist societies. Similarly, many men's acceptance of an ethics of rights, which focuses on the conflicts between people beyond 'the personal sphere', attaching primary value to the individual and his ability to pursue his own goals, becomes intelligible on the supposition that they have a sense of self in terms of separation only: the sense of self Chodorow's account says men develop as a result of growing up in families in which only women mother and are devalued.

Let me expand on how a Chodorowian theory can explain why many men have a tendency to accept an ethics of rights. Gilligan's own characterization of an ethics of rights is sketchy,[64] but I think that the following general features are faithful to her understanding of most of what it includes, and incorporate some of the aspects discussed in section 1 of this chapter:

(1) An ethics of rights thinks that the need for morality and politics arises primarily from the fact that we have goals or life-plans that *diverge irreconcilably*. (The key project for moral and political theory, from this perspective, is to provide some conception – ideally a theory – of how conflicts between persons should be resolved.)[65]

(2) An ethics of rights assumes that we will be *indifferent* to each other's plans when these do not vitally affect our own.

(3) An ethics of rights attaches minimal importance to bonds between people beyond the personal sphere and so it has a weak commitment to the value of community.[66] It may, however, attach significant value to relations between friends, lovers and family.

(4) An ethics of rights sees the primary source of value within a

---

[64] Gilligan's primary concern is with an ethics of care because she believes that this has been neglected by those who have worked on moral development.

[65] Note that liberal and 'libertarian' political theory has been primarily concerned with issues such as when it is justified for a person, or group of people, to prevent another from doing what they want; what, if any, are the conditions under which a state has the right to enforce its decisions; what rights an individual has against others, including the state.

[66] In this respect, an ethics of rights is no different from a pure ethics of care: both attach minimal or no value to community.

person's life as his pursuit of his goals or projects. (A variety of different but mutually compatible reasons could be given for why this is important: the realization of one's goals might be regarded as valuable; the pursuit of these goals might be considered valuable in itself; the fact that they are one's own goals might be regarded as important.)

In short, we might say that an ethics of rights embodies a conception of the person according to which persons have wills or interests that are usually indifferent or irreconcilably opposed, and on which what is of primary value within a person's life is his pursuit of his goals.

We can now see how to explain more fully many men's acceptance of an ethics of rights in terms of a Chodorowian theory of gender construction. Because they continue to have the sense of self they acquire during infancy, i.e. a sense of self in terms of separation only, the following is true of them. Firstly, they are unwilling to change their own plans to fit in with those of others, e.g. to make compromises which would resolve conflicts. And they observe that this is true of many other men too, so believe that, for the most part, people have plans that are irreconcilable. In consequence, they think that the most pressing problem for morality and politics is the adjudication of conflicting claims (see (1) above). Secondly, they view the plans of others primarily in terms of whether these help or hinder their ability to pursue their own; when there is no personal connection involved, they are indifferent to others. Their limited capacity for imaginative understanding reinforces their tendency towards indifference. They also observe that this tendency is possessed by many other men as well, so they conclude that persons in general will be indifferent to the plans of those to whom they are not personally affiliated, except when these impinge upon their own (see (2) above). Thirdly, within their lives they attach primary value to the pursuit of their own goals; they conclude that it is each individual's pursuit of his own goals which is of primary value in human life in general and of primary significance for morality and politics (see (4) above).

These links between possession of a sense of self in terms of separation and acceptance of an ethics of rights exploit a mechanism according to which persons introspect and make judgements (which may be mistaken) about their own attitudes, and then observe others, coming to the conclusion that others are similar to what they judge themselves to be like;[67] men observe other *men* and come to the conclusion that most *people* have the properties that are characteristic of the possession of a sense of self in terms of separation. This blindness to women, and women's experience, itself stands in need of explanation, but its existence is well documented by much recent feminist theory, which has drawn attention to the way in which women's experience has been ignored, or construed as truncated male experience. (Gilligan's own research is a contribution to this enterprise.) Gilligan's research supplements Chodorow's by giving us an account of how the initial senses of self that are acquired during infancy may nevertheless be transformed by personal experiences that are themselves structured or created by the sexual division of labour, even though they tend to be reinforced by it.

Chodorow's theory, coupled with Gilligan's, can, I suggest, explain a *variety* of different moral and political disagreements. It can construe some moral and political disputes between men and women in one of the following ways:

(1) As disputes between women (with a sense of self in terms of connection only) who reason according to an ethics of care, and men (with a sense of self in terms of separation only) who reason according to an ethics of rights;

(2) As disputes between women (with a sense of self in terms of connection and separation) who reason according to an ethics of care transformed by an ethics of rights, and men (with a sense of self in terms of separation only) who reason according to an ethics of rights;

(3) As disputes between men (with a sense of self in terms of separation and connection) who reason according to an ethics of rights transformed by an ethics of care, and women (with a sense of self in terms of connection only) who reason according to an ethics of care.

It can construe some moral and political disputes between men:

(4) As disputes between those (with a sense of self in terms of

---

[67] Naomi Scheman places importance on the *insecure* nature of masculine identity when exploring the attraction of different kinds of individualism that occur throughout the history of Western philosophy (e.g. the assumption that, in some sense, psychological states attach to persons singly). Scheman suggests that men are not only attracted to such views because these views are 'factually descriptive' of themselves, but are also 'deeply motivated' to accept the truth of these views as the truth about themselves (see Scheman, 'Individualism and the Objects of Psychology', p. 235). Although this chapter has been influenced by her work, my explanatory model does not emphasize the idea that masculinity is, in general, acquired insecurely, although it is not inconsistent with it.

separation and connection) who reason according to an ethics of rights transformed by an ethics of care, and those (with a sense of self in terms of separation only) who reason according to an ethics of rights.

It can construe some disputes between women:

(5) As disputes between those (with a sense of self in terms of connection only) who reason according to an ethics of care, and those (with a sense of self in terms of connection and separation) who reason according to a transformed ethics of care.

It might also be possible to understand some disputes between morally mature men and women as occurring because it is impossible to integrate fully an ethics of care and an ethics of rights, so their initial starting points continue to influence their moral orientation (see section 1 of this chapter).

The proposed explanatory model does not predict that there will be a consensus amongst women and a consensus amongst men on moral and political matters.[68] Since the model allows for change in both men's and women's moral and political perspectives as a result of transformational experiences, it allows for differences amongst (as well as between) them. Indeed, it might even be possible to construe some political disagreement as a phenomenon that occurs between men (or women) who have the *same* sense of self but, because of personal experiences, resist to different degrees the tendency to accept those views they find attractive.

The model integrates rational and non-rational considerations because it is claimed that a person comes to regard a consideration they had previously thought irrelevant to a decision as significant, or to attach greater weight to a consideration they had previously thought to be of minor importance, as a result of transformational experiences (such as the crises experienced by women when they confront unwanted pregnancies, or damaging relationships).

The model is materialist because power relations between men and women play an important role in explaining the different psychologies (in my terms, senses of self) possessed by men and women. It is crucially male power – the status of men in the 'public world' – which makes it attractive for the boy to reject his mother and acquire his masculine roles by a denial of femininity, i.e. male

---

68 If it did predict such a consensus, this alone would be sufficient to cast doubt on the truth of the explanatory claim since there manifestly isn't a consensus amongst either men or women on moral or political matters (see Grimshaw, *Feminist Philosophers*, p. 168).

power contributes to his development of a sense of self in terms of separation; and it is male power which leads the girl to turn to her father and thereby enables her to develop a fuller sense of herself as distinct from (although of the same kind as) her mother. (The model also has another potentially materialist dimension. As I have presented it, there is room to explain the existence of the sexual division of labour and its reproduction partly by reference to coercive pressures that are a function of the power relations between men and women; and it is the sexual division of labour – in particular women's responsibility for mothering – which is crucial in the initial formation, and sometimes the later reinforcement, of the senses of self girls and boys acquire.)

4 AN APPLICATION OF THE MODEL: AN INDIVIDUALISTIC CONCEPTION OF SELF-ESTEEM

The applications of the explanatory model presented so far have been quite general, therefore in this section I propose to apply the model to explain the widespread acceptance of a particular view of self-esteem which is developed with great clarity in the work of a contemporary political philosopher, Robert Nozick.[69] This will involve integrating both rational and non-rational considerations. My suggestion is this: we can explain the widespread acceptance of a conception of self-esteem that is elucidated by Nozick if we understand the appeal of the arguments offered in its support to those with a sense of self in terms of separation only. I am not proposing that we can explain *Nozick's* acceptance of this conception in this way. A claim of that sort could be justified only by examining closely the whole network of moral and political arguments Nozick presents in *Anarchy, State and Utopia* and elsewhere. The conception of self-esteem that Nozick elucidates is not unique to him. I suggest that he has merely presented with greater articulacy a view that is part of popular consciousness, and the acceptance of which can be explained in many cases by the explanatory model I have developed.

According to Nozick, people acquire self-esteem by believing that they possess significant quantities of some talent or attribute which is valued by at least some others; in order to gain self-esteem, people

---

[69] The following discussion draws on my 'Nozick on Self-Esteem', *Journal of Applied Philosophy*, vol. 7, 1990, pp. 91–8.

must believe that they score highly along some dimension(s) which others also think important. Nozick claims that whether a person does score highly along a dimension is determined by what scores are achieved by *others*. Consider a talent for playing basketball:

a man living in an isolated mountain village can sink 15 jump shots with a basketball out of 150 tries. Everyone else in the village can sink only 1 jump shot out of 150 tries. He thinks (as do the others) that he's very good at it. One day along comes Jerry West.[70]

The general point Nozick wishes to make is that we judge how well we do things by comparing our performance to others. Taken as an empirical generalization about the way in which some people assess what they do, his claim has merit. However, on Nozick's account it is not merely a contingent fact that people often evaluate their performance by comparison with others; it is a necessary truth because 'there is no standard of doing something well, independent of how it is or can be done by others'.[71] With some activities such as basketball, and competitive games in general, Nozick's conceptual claim has plausibility. Consider the question of what it is to play chess well. It seems that there is no standard apart from how others play chess. A league table of chess players could be drawn up and how well a person plays chess would be determined by the position she occupies in that table or some relevant part of it.

But as Anthony Skillen notes with respect to many other activities (such as those which have an independent product), Nozick's claim that there is no non-comparative standard of doing something well is inaccurate. It is at best a distortion based on a generalization from a one-sided diet of examples and at worst straightforwardly false:[72]

a boat either floats or it doesn't, a fishing net either holds or it doesn't, people can either do mouth-to-mouth resuscitation or they cannot, and such things are valued without the need for point-scoring and all the paraphernalia of winning and losing with which Nozick is so preoccupied.[73]

[70] Nozick, *Anarchy, State, and Utopia*, p. 240.
[71] *Ibid.*, p. 241.
[72] Nozick does allow that there may be some dimensions along which it is 'inappropriate to judge oneself comparatively', e.g. holiness and wisdom. But he regards these as peripheral phenomena and hence of limited sociological interest (see *Anarchy, State and Utopia*, p. 244).
[73] A. Skillen, *Ruling Illusions: Philosophy and the Social Order* (Hassocks, Sussex: Harvester, 1977), p. 49. My views have been strongly influenced by Skillen's discussion.

Nozick might admit that there are criteria which do not involve an implicit comparison with the performance of others, and which are relevant in the assessment of how well someone has performed an activity like building a boat. But he might go on to insist that satisfaction of these criteria alone is never sufficient to determine whether an activity has been performed well. Is ending up with a boat that doesn't sink sufficient to show that a craftsman has performed the activity of building a boat well? In this spirit, Nozick might argue against Skillen that building a boat well requires not merely that one builds a boat, but also that one builds a *good* boat. He might then claim that what it is to build a good boat cannot be specified independently of the achievements of others. But this is highly questionable: boats have a function and there seems no reason to deny that what it is to build a good boat can be spelt out purely by reference to this function.

Even if it were correct that a full analysis of, e.g. what it is to build a good boat, would reveal an interpersonal comparison at some point, this would not mean that gaining self-esteem must involve comparative judgements. We can make a distinction between performing an activity *successfully* and performing an activity *well*. In many cases it is clear that performing an activity successfully does not involve a reference to the achievements of others and provides a basis for self-esteem, so a person may acquire self-esteem without believing that they have performed some activity better than others. I may achieve my aim of building a boat merely by constructing a vessel that floats; this achievement may be sufficient for me to acquire self-esteem even when I recognize that others could have built a better boat.

This suggests that there is generally a non-comparative consideration from which it is possible (in principle) for a person to derive self-esteem: namely, whether the aims and objectives he or she had in performing an activity have been fulfilled. Suppose that most people build boats that last twenty years, whereas I build one that lasts only twelve months. It may seem that I haven't been successful, but if I only intended to build a boat that would last me a year, then I have successfully done what I meant to do. In contrast, suppose I try to build a boat that will serve me as long as possible, yet someone else with the same materials builds a boat that lasts nineteen years longer than mine. This would show that I hadn't been successful, but this would be because I manifestly haven't achieved what I wanted, not because someone did better than I.

Nozick rejects the idea that one might create a society in which no-one suffers from low self-esteem by downgrading the importance of dimensions that are socially valued or by equalizing scores along those dimensions. Initially he maintains that it is likely that some new dimension would come to be regarded as important and those who did badly along it would, again, come to have a low sense of self-worth.[74] Later Nozick goes further and suggests that there is an incoherence in the very idea that one might eradicate low self-esteem by equalizing scores along different dimensions: in Nozick's view, self-esteem must be based on differentiating characteristics (i.e. characteristics in which persons differ from others), so if everyone performed equally well along those dimensions that are regarded as important, these dimensions could no longer provide self-esteem for anyone. Hence such a policy would result in universally low self-esteem.[75]

According to Nozick, how much self-esteem is available will depend on how many dimensions exist that are valued by at least some. In his view, the best way to increase levels of self-esteem is to change people's attitudes so that they come to value many different sorts of activities and weight the value of these activities differently;[76] reforms to social and economic institutions, for example, are not likely to improve levels of self-esteem:

The most promising ways for a society to avoid widespread differences in self-esteem would be to have no common weighting of dimensions; instead it would have a diversity of different lists of dimensions and weightings. This would enhance each person's chance of finding dimensions that some others also think important, along which he does reasonably well, and so to make a non-idiosyncratic favorable estimate of himself.[77]

So in Nozick's view if there are only a limited number of dimensions that are significantly valued in a society, self-esteem will be limited: under these circumstances, it is likely that one person's self-esteem will result in another person's sense of worthlessness.

[74] Nozick, *Anarchy, State and Utopia*, p. 243.
[75] *Ibid.*, p. 245.
[76] He might consistently have added that levels of self-esteem could be improved by educating people so that they do not rely on the judgements of others as to the worth of what they do – unless he thinks this is psychologically impossible.
[77] Nozick, *Anarchy, State and Utopia*, pp. 245–6.

Inevitably envy will be rife because each person will have a reason for wanting to do better than others along these dimensions so that their own self-esteem is enhanced. If on the other hand there are a considerable number of dimensions along which persons can acquire self-esteem (i.e. a number of activities or attributes that are valued by at least some people), then self-esteem may not be a zero-sum game and, indeed, it may be the case that no-one suffers from low self-esteem. A person will still be threatened by others, however, since they may decide to take up some activity from which he derives self-esteem and do it better, thereby making it more difficult for him to gain self-esteem from it. In consequence, a person always has an interest that is opposed to others taking up the activities from which he or she derives self-esteem if these others are likely to perform them better, and always has an interest that is furthered by other people taking up and performing poorly in these activities so he or she can preserve or enhance self-esteem.[78]

The story about how persons acquire self-esteem which Nozick tells involves the idea that people must make comparative judgements in order to acquire self-esteem and that people's interests in gaining self-esteem are necessarily opposed. The story I have implicitly told in opposition to Nozick's maintains that people need not make comparative judgements in order to gain self-esteem and that there is no *necessary* conflict of interests in the acquisition of self-esteem. When there is a conflict of interests over its acquisition, this is because of the way in which people, as a matter of fact, gain self-esteem: people may derive self-esteem from making comparative judgements and believing that they are better than others in some valued respect. But this is not part of the *nature* of self-esteem.

Gilligan's research suggests that in general men and women gain self-esteem in different ways. She concludes that 'women not only define themselves in a context of relationship, but also judge themselves in terms of their ability to care'.[79] In contrast, 'instead of attachment, individual achievement rivets the male imagination, and great ideas or distinctive activity define the standard of self-assessment and success'.[80] Men often come to value activities which

---

[78] Cf. Nozick's suggestion that a person who thinks that he is good at basketball or mathematics 'might prefer that other persons lacked their talents, or prefer that they stop continually demonstrating their worth, at least in front of him; that way his self-esteem will avoid battering and can be shored up' (*Anarchy, State and Utopia*, p. 241).

[79] Gilligan, *In a Different Voice*, p. 17; see p. 70.

[80] *Ibid.*, p. 163.

are impersonal: some of these activities are essentially competitive and most lend themselves easily to comparative judgements. In contrast, women come to value 'person-oriented' activities, such as caring for others, success at which is not naturally nor easily measured by comparison with the performance of others. (Gilligan also cites evidence that women are threatened by competitive success,[81] so on these grounds it seems unlikely that they would acquire self-esteem, say, by believing that they were able to care more deeply than others.)

I propose that the interest in, and attraction of, the view that the making of comparative judgements is essential in order to gain self-esteem, and that there must be a conflict of interests over the acquisition of self-esteem, can be explained by Chodorow's theory of gender construction: because many men have a sense of self in terms of separation only, they will tend to find considerations which invoke or presuppose such a conception of how one person stands in relation to another attractive. The mechanism linking the possession of a sense of self in terms of separation with the acceptance of this sort of conception of self-esteem can be plausibly represented as follows: men with such a sense of self introspect, and observe other men, coming to the conclusion that people acquire self-esteem by judging themselves to be better than others in valued respects. They are blind to the possibility of gaining self-esteem by other means and inflate a factual claim (with limited truth) to the status of a conceptual truth.

In the last section of this chapter, I tried to give an illustration of how the core of the explanatory model developed in the previous sections could be applied to explain the appeal of a particular conception of self-esteem. I wish to remain agnostic on the scope of the explanatory model. The process of uncovering the kind of individualism I have distinguished can be a demanding one, as I hope I have shown. Different political arguments, whether presented by academic political theorists, or by those who theorize about politics outside of academic contexts, may not display it openly. The fact that some argument or theory does presuppose such an individualism does not by itself demonstrate that its appeal rests on it nor (even when it does give reason for thinking that this is the source of its appeal) that the attractiveness of the theory to some can

---

[81] *Ibid.*, pp. 15–16.

be explained by the mechanisms I have suggested. But Gilligan's and Chodorow's research gives us some grounds in some cases for thinking that this is so. My claims on this matter, like theirs, have the status of bold conjectures rather than well-confirmed hypotheses.

Concluding remarks

Part of the interest in explaining why political disagreement is so intractable is to arrive at some assessment of the prospects for resolving it. In the introduction I distinguished between contestability and imperfection conceptions of how we should explain the intractability and pervasiveness of political disagreement. According to the imperfection conception, political disputes could in principle be settled to the satisfaction of any reasonable person who has the time and patience, and is able to apply the laws of logic fully and correctly; the contestability conception denies this because it holds that the rational constraints which govern the application of key political terms permit a range of different political viewpoints. The imperfection conception might seem to be inherently more optimistic than the contestability conception about the prospects of achieving a consensus without the use of coercive or manipulative means. But that appearance is merely superficial: defenders of the imperfection conception may with perfect consistency express deep scepticism about the possibility of rationally resolving political disputes in practice. Optimism is appropriate within the imperfection conception only if the barriers to rational consensus are regarded as removable; and lack of clarity, vested interests, the role of passion in clouding the perception of moral and political truth, limited human ability or the sheer difficulty in arriving at it given the complexity of the moral and political world, might be thought to place insuperable obstacles in the way of achieving a consensus on moral and political matters in practice. Some versions of the imperfection conception may also be optimistic about the chances of convergence in one context but not in another. Locke's version, for example, was optimistic about the possibility of reaching agreement within moral and political philosophy but pessimistic about the possibility of achieving the necessary clarity for such convergence within ordinary life.

What does the conception I have defended, which incorporates elements from both the imperfection and contestability conceptions, imply about the prospects of convergence on a body of moral and political beliefs? It suggests that we have no reason to *expect* convergence on central issues, such as which conception of justice should govern our main institutions. There is a diversity of influences in advanced capitalist societies and these tend to exert different kinds of pressures on belief formation. Major institutions, such as the family, act as a unifying force to some extent because they have a tendency to affect particular groups of people in the same way, but we should not expect them to provide the conditions for a consensus on key moral and political questions. Even if each of us were fully autonomous in judgement (i.e. if our judgements could be fully explained simply by reference to the reasons we have for making them), there would still be scope for disagreement provided various other conditions continued to obtain, e.g. there continued to be some measure of freedom of expression, consensus carried on being a secondary rather than a primary aim of moral and political discourse, and the reach of intellectual authority remained short.

Rawls's optimism about the possibility of an overlapping consensus on a particular conception of justice therefore seems misplaced. His reasons for thinking that such a consensus would be valuable are appealing nonetheless. An overlapping consensus would make possible the *public justification* of our major institutions: citizens would be able to justify to each other the institutions which govern their lives. That seems valuable in itself, provided that we add to Rawls's account the qualification that the consensus must be on a correct conception of justice in order for public justification to be worthwhile (see introduction); furthermore, as Rawls maintains, public justification is likely to make democratic societies more enduring and stable. Others besides Rawls have also emphasized the importance of public justification: Charles Larmore has in effect argued in favour of it on the basis of 'a universal norm of rational dialogue'.[1] This norm amounts to a 'commitment to converse rationally about what ought to be collectively binding political principles'.[2] Larmore supposes that when there is disagreement over what principles should govern state policy, it should not be resolved by the coercive

[1] See C. Larmore, *Patterns of Moral Complexity* (Cambridge: Cambridge University Press, 1987), p. 53.
[2] *Ibid.*, p. 54.

imposition of one set of disputed principles; it should be settled by rational argument instead.

Public justifiability of major institutions perhaps rests upon a weaker condition and doesn't require an overlapping consensus on a particular conception of justice, viz. the condition that the justification for these institutions should appeal only to a common, objective or impersonal method of reasoning. If such a method could justify a particular conception of justice, it does not follow that everyone would, as a matter of fact, converge on it; however, the idea would be that in so far as they did not converge upon it, the explanation for this failure of convergence would include the idea that they had applied or interpreted the method imperfectly.[3] This would fit an imperfection conception of how disagreements over which conception of justice is correct are to be explained: people disagree over conceptions of justice because they are limited, imperfect creatures who make errors of reasoning, or fail to consider all the evidence which (by their own lights as well) is relevant. Again, however, it is not clear that a particular conception of justice could be justified by such a method: if 'justice' is an essentially contested concept, there will be no such method even though there may be a uniquely correct conception of justice; the discovery of this conception requires a kind of judgement the correctness of which cannot be demonstrated simply by appealing to common methods of reasoning, i.e. premises and rules of inference that all reasonable people share.

Public justifiability may be attainable in degrees, even if its full realization is impossible in practice. In the absence of convergence on a particular conception of social justice, or even on a method for settling disputes over which conception is correct, there may still be significant agreement on acceptable *procedures* for determining the design of major institutions and for fashioning state policy: in liberal democracies, for example, there will be general agreement that these procedures should be democratic and that citizens should be equal before the law. Of course, there is likely to be considerable disagreement about what constitutes an ideally democratic procedure and over what pieces of legislation are compatible with equality before the law; however, there should be enough agreement on the minimal conditions which need to be met by a procedure for it to

---

[3] Cf. T. Nagel, 'Moral Conflict and Political Legitimacy', *Philosophy and Public Affairs*, vol. 16, 1987, especially p. 235.

count as democratic, and for a law to treat people as equals, to allow some degree of public justification of legislation and policy in a society that meets these conditions.

Even if public justifiability is an ideal partially out of reach, there are reasons for thinking that democratic regimes may be stable without its full realization. Whether a consensus on procedures is enough for a democratic regime to be stable will depend upon specific features of the regime in question. It will depend, for example, on the history of the relations between the different groups within it; whether, for example, they have been characterized primarily by exploitation, hostility and oppression, or by mutual respect and justice. Consensus on procedures may, in some circumstances, provide a sufficient basis for stability but that will surely depend in part upon the extent to which members of currently or previously disadvantaged groups judge that their grievances are being, or indeed can be, genuinely addressed under current arrangements. And, of course, their perceptions here will be informed by conceptions of justice and fairness on which we have no reason to expect consensus. When relations have been or are oppressive, 'principles of accommodation', such as the one David Wong recommends, viz. that people act on their moral and political positions 'in a way that minimizes potential damage to [their] broader relationship to others who have opposed positions',[4] may be irrelevant or redundant if those who have been or continue to be oppressed judge that there is no worthwhile relationship there to preserve.

Principles of accommodation no doubt would (and do) provide a valuable way of coping with moral and political conflict when relationships between those with opposed positions are relatively healthy. Amy Gutmann and Dennis Thompson have argued that we need principles of this kind to govern the conduct of debates, so that disagreement is conducted in an atmosphere of mutual respect: '[m]utual respect ... requires an effort to appreciate the moral force of the positions of people with whom we disagree'.[5] They claim that this involves (amongst other things) acknowledging the moral *status* of our opponents' positions by refraining from treating their arguments as purely non-moral, economic or confused, and requires that

---

[4] D. Wong, 'Coping with Moral Conflict and Ambiguity', *Ethics*, vol. 102, 1992, p. 777.

[5] A. Gutmann and D. Thompson, 'Moral Conflict and Political Consensus', *Ethics*, vol. 101, 1990, p. 85.

we 'search for significant points of convergence between our own understandings and those of citizens whose positions, taken in their more comprehensive forms, we must reject'.[6] Satisfaction of these conditions, and others like them, would require not only changes in attitudes amongst those engaged in debate but also institutional changes.[7] One legitimate complaint radicals have made against advanced capitalist societies is that these contain insufficient possibilities for the advocacy of unorthodox political viewpoints. There is a case to be made that authentic mutual respect requires the provision of media time and space for the airing of radical or unusual arguments, not merely the absence of legal or other constraints on their expression.

Again, however, we should not be too optimistic about the full attainment of a state of affairs in which this kind of mutual respect flourishes and is fostered by institutions. It is possible to acknowledge the moral *status* of a position but believe that it is nevertheless wholly mistaken and not the kind of position over which genuine argument can take place. This is often the stance of opponents of abortion who regard defenders of it as morally corrupt and incapable of responding to moral considerations. Gutmann and Thompson criticize dogmatic contributors to the abortion debate, whether they be 'pro-choice' or 'pro-life', for refusing to recognize the reasonableness of their opponents' positions. But of course those they have in mind would simply deny that the standpoint of their opponents *is* reasonable. Gutmann and Thompson underestimate the depth of disagreement over which positions within a debate are disputable; they think it relatively easy to show that different reasonable viewpoints are available on issues such as abortion and capital punishment, that it is unreasonable to suppose that one's own opinion is the only reasonable viewpoint. But disagreement over which positions are reasonable is often just as intractable as disagreement over which position is correct.

Much the same problem is of course faced in *identifying* a concept as essentially contested: take any key political concept and there will be those who argue that their own use of the concept is uniquely reasonable and can be demonstrated by the application of a common method of reasoning. To show that they are mistaken in holding this view, someone who defends the identification of a

[6] *Ibid.*, p. 82.
[7] *Ibid.*, p. 85.

concept as essentially contested will need to *engage* in political debate. Identifying a concept as essentially contested is not some neutral act of 'describing language-games'; it is in part to make a non-neutral judgement about which uses of a concept are reasonable. For example, some libertarians argue that socialists who include need as a criterion of justice simply confuse justice with charity; they deny that the satisfaction of basic needs can be reasonably regarded as a requirement of justice. Those who think that justice is an essentially contestable concept because its proper application is governed by a number of different criteria,[8] including need, have to defend the view that considerations of need are relevant to questions of justice. This is not something which can be achieved *simply* by describing actual usage, for that is exactly what is being disputed.

The value of public justifiability and of stability gives us reason for worrying about the extent and persistence of contemporary moral and political disagreement, and gives us reason for seeking principles of accommodation of the kind that Wong and Gutmann and Thompson are concerned to find, but it is important not to overlook some of the beneficial consequences of the existence of moral and political differences. John Stuart Mill emphasized the value of engaging in debate with others who adhere to different moral and political positions from our own. He supposed that a large proportion of our reasons for holding any moral and political belief must consist in arguments for rejecting the alternatives because on these matters: '... three-fourths of the arguments for every disputed opinion consist in dispelling the appearances which favour some opinion different from it'.[9] Mill concluded that a person can hold her views on moral and political views rationally only if she takes part in arguments with those who are committed to opposing positions. This classical liberal belief in the importance of autonomous thought and the way in which it should be fostered through debate is not incompatible with the contemporary liberal belief in the importance of public justifiability through a consensus of some sort, but it would be naive to suppose that they can be easily reconciled when it comes to implementing policy and legitimizing it, even with the help of principles of accommodation.

[8] See D. Miller, *Social Justice* (Oxford: Oxford University Press, 1976).
[9] J. S. Mill, *On Liberty* (New York: Bobbs-Merrill, 1956), p. 44.

Appendix

The explanatory model developed in chapter 5 relies heavily on Nancy Chodorow's theory of the construction of gender and Carol Gilligan's account of gender differences in moral reasoning. Both of these have been subject to criticism. In this appendix I propose to consider what can be said in response to the objections to their work which are the most relevant to my project.

PART I: ON SOME CRITICISMS OF CHODOROW'S THEORY OF GENDER CONSTRUCTION

In the first part of this appendix I shall consider what I take to be the most pertinent criticisms of Chodorow's theory of how masculinity and femininity are acquired: firstly, the claim that the psychoanalytic concepts out of which it is constructed are problematic because the evidence for their empirical applicability is weak; secondly, the objection that Chodorow's thesis implies that persons are socially determined and as a result leaves no room for individual autonomy; thirdly, the criticism that her theory is insensitive to, and cannot explain, variations in gender identity through time, between cultures, or across race and class; fourthly, the claim that Chodorow's theory ignores structural constraints which, for example, explain why women come to mother and to occupy the particular gender roles they do.

1 Infantile sexuality, the unconscious and sex-role socialization theories

Psychoanalytic accounts of gender development, such as Chodorow's, encounter general difficulties in relation to the two key notions that are definitive of them, viz. the unconscious and infantile sexuality. Although these notions seem coherent, the question of

147

whether they are empirically applicable, i.e. whether infants really do have sexual desires, and whether each of us really does have an unconscious, is difficult; any answer to it is bound to be deeply controversial. Freud maintains that the contents of the unconscious can be known but only through a complex set of interpretive rules that allow psychoanalysts to 'decode' speech, dreams and symptoms. He argues that the memories of the sexual desires we had as infants are repressed into the unconscious; he considers our lack of memory of experiencing sexual desire when we were infants to be evidence for his theory, which gives rise to the fear that it is not merely irrefutable[1] but uncriticizable. Observations of children's behaviour and the interpretation of the dreams, speech and behaviour of adults might provide evidence for infantile sexuality, but these observations and interpretations only count as evidence in the context of some set of interpretive rules which themselves stand in need of justification.

Since claims about the contents of the unconscious and about infantile sexuality are inherently controversial, there are advantages in attempting to reconstruct Chodorow's theory so that it does not depend upon them (but on the other hand remains consistent with them). It is fortunate that her account can be reformulated in such a way that it needn't affirm or deny the theory of infantile sexuality, nor the theory of the unconscious which she endorses. The early relationships between mother and child, and father and daughter, can be regarded as sensual and emotionally significant, whilst remaining agnostic on the further question of whether they are sexually charged from the infant's point of view. Chodorow could also perhaps do without a theory of the unconscious. If gender is irreversibly acquired by the age of three, as the evidence suggests, we need some account of how a psychological orientation that is gained so early can have such deep effects on adult life. On Freudian accounts, this is explained by appealing to the way in which early experiences structure the unconscious, whose contents remain relatively permanent over time, but there may be alternative mechanisms that can better explain the pervasive effects of infantile experience on later life. So there would perhaps be no need to endorse any claims about the existence and contents of the Freudian unconscious.[2]

---

[1] See K. Popper, *Conjectures and Refutations: The Growth of Scientific Knowledge* (London: Routledge and Kegan Paul, 1963) p. 37.

[2] Some psychoanalytic theorists, such as Jacqueline Rose, would deny that a theory of the unconscious does anyway play a significant role in Chodorow's account (and would regard

Chodorow's account, purged of its controversial notions of the unconscious and infantile sexuality, is not psychoanalytic any longer, but it retains much of its original shape. Chodorow herself acknowledges that the evidence she gives for her theory is not restricted to the kind of evidence relevant to a specifically psycho-analytic account; it goes beyond the interpretation of speech, dreams and symptoms.[3] It might be objected, however, that the account which remains, when the psychoanalytic content of the theory is purged, is no different from sex-role socialization accounts which include mechanisms for the learning of sex roles by identifi-cation. Even though Chodorow's theory reconstructed in this way is compatible with sex-role socialization models, it still differs from standard versions of them because it maintains that a person's fittedness for the performance of a particular gender role is deter-mined by his or her sense of self.

Feminists who embrace psychoanalytic theories tend to be hostile to sex-role socialization accounts of gender construction because they think that these accounts do not go deep enough.[4] They argue that such accounts must suppose that there is an ungendered self which is the occupant of gender roles; psychoanalytic accounts, in contrast, maintain that we are gendered to the core. Sex-role sociali-zation theories need not suppose that each man and woman has an ungendered self, however: the superficial grammatical form of these theories may suggest such a commitment but their basic structure allows that persons are thoroughly gendered, and that this is what fits them to perform the specific roles to which they are assigned by society.

What then would distinguish an account, such as Chodorow's, if it were purged of its psychoanalytic theory of the unconscious and infantile sexuality? Chodorow emphasizes the fact that gender is acquired by the age of three. Standard sex-role socialization models do not explain this, since they view role-training and identification as something that occurs after this age. This is not evidence for an

this as a deficiency in it). It is certainly true that in displacing the Oedipus complex from the centre of an account of gender construction, and focusing attention on the pre-Oedipal phase, it becomes unclear exactly what is transformed and repressed into the unconscious to produce senses of self in terms of separation or connection (see J. Mitchell and J. Rose eds, *Feminine Sexuality: Jacques Lacan and the Ecole Freudienne* (London: Macmillan, 1982), p. 37).

[3] J. Lorber, R. Laub Coser, A. S. Rossi, and N. Chodorow, 'On *The Reproduction of Mothering*: A Methodological Debate', *Signs: Journal of Women in Culture and Society*, vol. 6, 1981, p. 505.

[4] See J. Sayers, *Sexual Contradictions: Psychology, Psychoanalysis and Feminism* (London: Rout-ledge, 1986), p. 31.

account which employs psychoanalytic notions, however, since the early acquisition of gender might be explicable in terms of the differential treatment of male and female infants without appealing to such conceptions. Indeed, the differential treatment involved could, it seems to me, be construed as sex-role socialization since it provides the basis from which girls and boys acquire sex roles. If this is correct, the theory I have outlined which purges Chodorow's account of its conceptions of the unconscious and infantile sexuality, is one kind of sex-role socialization theory.

2 Personal autonomy and the construction of gender

Some commentators have criticized Chodorow on the grounds that her theory denies the possibility of any genuine individual autonomy. For example, Jean Elshtain writes:

Human subjects are constituted by Chodorow's discourse as objectified role-players, turned out as over-socialized beings stuck in a rigid 'sex-gender system and sexual asymmetry' . . . The human subject as a desiring, fantasizing, self-defining agent is lost. Children are human clay awaiting their molding into 'gendered members of society'.[5]

Pace Elshtain, it may be that individual possibilities for change are quite constrained, especially if (as I suggested in chapter 5) the major institutions, such as the family, the market and private property, tend, in general, to reinforce the gendered senses of self acquired during infancy. Chodorow needn't be read as denying the possibility of any significant individual autonomy, however. Admittedly she sometimes speaks as if she were denying this possibility. For example, she says that 'object relations theorists argue that the child's social relational experience from earliest infancy is determining for psychological growth and personality formation'[6] and that 'the Oedipus complex thus engenders splits in the ego and its object world that come to constitute a basic fixing of personality'.[7] But one paragraph after the place at which this second claim appears, Chodorow writes:

5 J. Elshtain, 'Symmetry and Soporifics: A Critique of Feminist Accounts of Gender Development' in B. Richards (ed) *Capitalism and Infancy: Essays on Psychoanalysis and Politics* (London: Free Association Books, 1984), p. 74. Cf. T. Moi, 'Patriarchal Thought and the Drive for Knowledge' in T. Brennan (ed) *Between Feminism and Psychoanalysis* (London: Routledge, 1989), p. 191.
6 Chodorow, *The Reproduction of Mothering*, p. 47.
7 *Ibid.*, pp. 163–4.

This final Oedipal stance, because it is now unconscious and was conceived at a period when the child felt particularly helpless and vulnerable, continues to exert a powerful influence in later life. Further change in a person's inner ego and object-world and sense of relational self can certainly take place after the Oedipal period, especially at times which reawaken and bring to prominence a complex of major life-cycle relations and social definitions.[8]

Also when she explicitly confronts the question of psychological determination, she remarks:

Psychoanalysis does show that we are formed in crucial ways by the time we are five, but it allows for change, either from life experiences or through the analytic process ... Psychoanalysis, moreover, argues against a unilateral model of social determination, and for the variation and creativity in what people make of their early childhood experiences and other experiences as well.[9]

Using these passages to illuminate the others, we can read Chodorow as accepting that the pre-Oedipal mother-child relationship, and the Oedipal triangles, do not rigidly constrain the individual even though they tend to have deep effects on later life.[10] The explanatory model developed in chapter 5 appeals to Gilligan's idea that a person's sense of self may be transformed in response to crises: these may lead a person to change their conception of how they stand in relation to others and thereby result in personal change. Chodorow's account, as I interpret it, has space for this idea.

3 Is Chodorow's theory insensitive to variations in gender identity?

Some critics have argued that Chodorow's account is insensitive to cultural differences[11] and variations in gender identity across race and class. Those with postmodernist sympathies have criticized Chodorow's theory for being 'essentialist', on the grounds that it treats mothering as a cultural universal.[12] If my reading of Chodorow is correct, however, this objection is misconceived as it stands.

---

[8] *Ibid.*, p. 164.
[9] *Ibid.*, pp. 216–17.
[10] This interpretation of Chodorow is not idiosyncratic; Sandra Harding, for example, also offers it (see Harding, 'What is the Real Material Base of Patriarchy and Capital?', p. 147).
[11] See J. Elshtain, 'Symmetry and Soporifics'; J. Sayers, 'Psychoanalysis and Personal Politics: A Response to Elizabeth Wilson', *Feminist Review*, vol. 10, 1982, pp. 91–5.
[12] See N. Fraser and L. J. Nicholson, 'Social Criticism without Philosophy: An Encounter between Feminism and Postmodernism' in L. J. Nicholson (ed) *Feminism/Postmodernism* (London: Routledge, 1990) pp. 29–31.

Her theory does allow that the nature of mothering varies. It is intended to apply specifically to developed capitalist societies, and other societies that have relevantly similar features, viz. male dominance, father absence from the home, and only women involved in mothering. Postmodernists may be sceptical of theory which attempts to understand anything as broad as 'gender identity in developed capitalist societies' but I do not see how theorizing at this level of generality can be shown, a priori, to be misguided. More specific doubts of this kind might be raised against Chodorow, however. In an important discussion, which I think provides the most serious challenge to Chodorow's theory, Elizabeth Spelman argues that it treats gender, race and class as independent variables and fails to recognize the way in which a person's race or class may affect their gender identity;[13] she points out, for example, that a working-class woman's gender identity may differ from a middle-class woman's.

Chodorow's theory may well have the resources to meet this criticism, however. She implicitly distinguishes between two different stages of psychosexual development, viz. the acquisition of a *core* gender identity and the acquisition of a *full* gender identity.[14] (Spelman notes that Chodorow refers to core gender identity whilst also describing gender in more specific terms,[15] but does not explore the idea that these modes of description might mark a distinction implicit in Chodorow's account between two different stages of psychosexual development.) A child's core gender identity is its sense of fitting into a category either the same as, or different from, his or her primary caretaker. It is only later that children come to understand that they are male or female, and that the category they fit into is of great social significance because they are valued more or less as a result. Chodorow can certainly allow that a child or adult's full gender identity will be affected by (and will in turn affect) his or her class or ethnic identity. What it is for a white middle-class man to be masculine will be different from what it is for a white working-class man:[16] when a white middle-class boy or a white working-class

---

13 E. Spelman, *Inessential Woman: Problems of Exclusion in Feminist Thought* (London: Women's Press, 1990), ch. 4. Cf. P. Leonard, *Personality and Ideology: Towards a Materialist Understanding of the Individual* (London: Macmillan, 1984), p. 54.
14 See, e.g. Chodorow, *Feminism and Psychoanalytic Theory*, pp. 108–12.
15 See Spelman, *Inessential Woman*, p. 86; section 5.
16 The distinction between a person's core gender identity and his or her full gender identity may also help to answer the criticisms of those who have claimed that Chodorow represents

boy learns what it is to be masculine he does so, at least in part, by identifying with the *appropriate* cultural images of masculinity, which will often be class and race specific.

What of the core gender identity which a child acquires during infancy? Can Chodorow allow that this too is affected by the child's class and ethnic identity (if indeed he or she has one at this very early stage)? The nature of the relational triangle between child, mother, and father (when he is present) to which Chodorow appeals might vary between classes and ethnic groups: there may be vari-ations in the number of women involved in childcare, and in the extent to which the father is absent from the home. So the basic structure of Chodorow's theory is compatible with recognizing that a person's gender identity may be affected by the class or ethnic group to which he or she belongs.[17] If child-rearing practices do not vary along these dimensions, then it is quite plausible for Chodorow to maintain that any 'core' ethnic or class identity that the child acquires contemporaneously with his or her core gender identity will be largely independent of it.

Chodorow does seem to suppose that (in general, in developed capitalist societies) a person's initially acquired, core gender identity will be fundamentally preserved despite being incorporated into a full gender identity, the content of which will be determined by other factors such as race and class. That assumption stands in need of empirical support. Even if it is false, however, the structure of Chodorow's account (as I have interpreted it) allows that a person's initially acquired sense of self may be transformed by later experi-ences and hence recognizes that a person's core gender identity need not be fixed. To the extent that relevant transforming experiences are structured by factors such as race and class, Chodorow's theory allows the possibility that a person's core gender identity may come

female gender identity as easily achieved and hence non-conflictual (see J. Grimshaw, 'Masculinity, Femininity and Mothering', Hull Centre for Gender Studies, occasional paper no. 3, p. 20. M. Whitford, 'Representing Irigaray' in T. Brennan (ed) *Between Feminism and Psychoanalysis* (London: Routledge, 1989) p. 111). Core gender identity is, according to Chodorow's theory, non-conflictual, for a girl acquires it through an aware-ness of fitting into a category the same as her primary caretaker. Full gender identity, in contrast, is likely to be riddled with contradictions and unrealizable aspirations; it will not be unproblematic and comfortable.

[17] We should distinguish between the basic structure of Chodorow's theory and other remarks she makes about the relevance of race and class to gender identity; it is only if the basic structure of her theory is incompatible with a recognition of the way in which a person's gender identity is affected by her race and class that it is in deep trouble.

to be transformed as of result of these factors. The explanatory model developed in chapter 5 is simplified because it does not incorporate an account of how race and class affect moral and political reasoning, but the model could be refined in this way, and might then be used to explain a wider range of moral and political disagreements.

4 Structural constraints

In the context of a debate on *The Reproduction of Mothering*, Judith Lorber argues that 'in her emphasis on psychoanalytic interpretations, Chodorow neglects significant structural variables'.[18] In Lorber's view, it is *primarily* the separation of home from the market, and the income inequality between men and women, that leads women to become mothers rather than any sense of self they may acquire during infancy. Lorber's criticisms focus on the explanation Chodorow gives for why women come to mother but they have more general application and therefore threaten the use to which I have put Chodorow's theory. Lorber's argument might also be extended to suggest that masculinity and femininity are acquired primarily as a result of being forced to occupy particular positions within the division of labour which involve the exercise and development of certain psychological capacities at the expense of others.

Chodorow does often seem to neglect the importance of structural constraints in explaining how women become feminine and men masculine. But her theory also incorporates at least a potential recognition of them at a fundamental level, for she argues that the boy acquires his full masculine identity partly as a result of the devaluing of women and the valuing of men, reflected by the relative status of the two sexes in society, which is largely a consequence of the power structure which assigns women to the home or poorly paid jobs in the market, and men to the more highly paid ones. So her account requires a recognition of the structural constraints to which individual women are subject, even if it does not explain why, for example, women come to mother by appealing directly to these constraints. As Chodorow points out in her reply to Lorber, her concern is mainly with why women come to *want* to mother;[19] something which cannot be explained by a structural

18 Lorber *et al.*, 'On *The Reproduction of Mothering*: A Methodological Debate', p. 483.
19 *Ibid.*, p. 503.

account alone, for that merely reveals the barriers that make it the case that some women *have* to mother.[20]

The idea that the two sexes have a different relative status in society, and that this is a consequence of a power structure that governs their relations, is central to Chodorow's account. This makes it unclear what the theory predicts would happen to a particular child's gender identity were both its parents to be involved in mothering whilst the wider social context remained the same. So Chodorow's theory is not undermined by empirical evidence which suggests that under such arrangements children turn out little or no different from how they turn out under traditional child-rearing practices. Her prediction that if there was 'equal parenting', then 'masculinity would not become tied to denial of dependence and devaluation of women' and '[f]eminine personality would be less preoccupied with individuation',[21] applies to a society in which the power structure that pushes women towards the home or poorly paid jobs in the market, and men to the more highly paid ones, has been dismantled.

PART II: ON SOME PROBLEMS WITH GILLIGAN'S RESEARCH

Gilligan's research has been criticized on the grounds that her association of an ethics of care with women, and an ethics of rights with men, is insufficiently supported by the evidence. Some critics have also argued that even if we accept that women reason according to an ethics of care, this is best regarded as a means of coping with sexism rather than as a consequence of the sense of self they possess.

1 The evidence for Gilligan's hypothesis

Some commentators have argued that the grand conclusions Gilligan draws are not warranted by the data she has gathered. Gilligan would admit that she reaches her conclusions on the basis of only a

---

[20] Adrienne Rich also criticizes Chodorow on the grounds that she does not give any role to structural factors in explaining why girls become heterosexual. She contends that Chodorow must simply assume that women have an innate heterosexual orientation or that heterosexuality is simply a preference (Rich, 'Compulsory Heterosexuality and Lesbian Existence', p. 216). It is true that Chodorow doesn't give any extended discussion of the forces apart from the relational triangle between mother, father and daughter which pressurize and sometimes coerce girls to become heterosexual. But she needn't suppose that these forces are absent or that heterosexuality is chosen or innate.

[21] Chodorow, *The Reproduction of Mothering*, p. 218.

small number of interviews. The fact that she generalizes from a small sample does not show that her conclusions are false, however; it merely shows that they have the status of bold conjectures rather than well-confirmed hypotheses. Is there any evidence which undermines her conclusions?

In a survey of the psychological literature on sex differences in moral reasoning, Lawrence Walker contends that very few such differences have been found. But this claim needs to be understood in the context of Lawrence Kohlberg's theory of moral development: Walker's conclusion is that very few sex differences have been found in terms of progress through the six stage-sequence that Kohlberg's theory distinguishes. Gilligan does claim that Kohlberg's theory exhibits a bias against women but even if she is wrong on that question, it does not follow that there are no sex-related differences in moral reasoning. As Walker acknowledges:

the lack of stage-disparity in moral reasoning between males and females does not preclude the possibility of sex differences in content within a stage (e.g., reliance on particular norms) or in the preferential use of various orientations in the making of moral judgements.[22]

Gilligan's research does, however, ignore variables such as class and race.[23] Auerbach *et al.* have pointed out that in her abortion decision study she doesn't break down results by class, race, religion or ethnicity and that this is an important omission 'because such variables may be more important than gender in distinguishing patterns of decision making'. They suggest that the result of this omission is that 'Gilligan attributes all the differences she does encounter to gender'.[24] It is perhaps worth adding here that if gender identity varies across, e.g. class and race in the way Spelman suggests (see part I of this appendix), then there may be differences in moral reasoning which are due to differences in gender identity, created by differences in class or race, which Gilligan has failed to detect. Michelle Moody-Adams also points out that the excessive weight that Gilligan places on the abortion decision study is at the

---

[22] L. Walker, 'Sex Differences in the Development of Moral Reasoning: A Critical Review', *Child Development*, vol. 55, 1984, p. 688. Walker's analysis of the literature has been challenged: see D. Baumrind, 'Sex Differences in Moral Reasoning: Response to Walker's (1984) Conclusion That There Are None', *Child Development*, vol. 57, 1986, pp. 511–21. Walker replies to Baumrind in the same volume.

[23] See L. J. Nicholson, 'Women, Morality and History', *Social Research*, vol. 50, 1983, p. 530.

[24] J. Auerbach, L. Blum, V. Smith and C. Williams, 'Commentary on Gilligan's *In a Different Voice*', *Feminist Studies*, vol. 11, 1985, p. 155.

expense of considering a wider variety of circumstances in which women are confronted with difficult choices. She suggests that the dominance of 'care reasoning' that Gilligan finds in her female subjects may be 'a function of the kinds of problems they were asked (or not asked) about rather than a function of the way they actually think'.[25] Criticisms such as these again show that Gilligan's conclusions have to be understood as tentative proposals that future research may confirm or undermine, but do not refute them.

Some have also criticized Gilligan for her 'selective' use of material to support the hypotheses she advances. John Broughton examined in detail the transcript of an interview she conducted with one woman and came to the conclusion that it included both kinds of reasoning Gilligan distinguishes, although Gilligan only draws attention to one kind – the ethic of care.[26] Debra Nails argues that Gilligan's analysis of an interview with a woman she calls 'Betty' is also marred by a selectivity which makes the changes Betty undergoes seem more marked than they are.[27] In any presentation of research of the kind which Gilligan is doing, there is a need to select particular pieces of material to support conclusions that are drawn, and this material has to be interpreted. On this level, Nails is surely wrong when she appears to counterpose 'empirical science' with 'interpretation', implying that interpretation is a form of literary criticism (which, in Gilligan's case at least, Nails believes cannot be trusted). All social science interprets, although in so far as it is reliable and trustworthy, the interpretations have to be measured against all the data under consideration; if data exists which is inconsistent with the proposed interpretation, then this should at least be noted. How far Gilligan's research in general is 'selective' in the undesirable sense of that term, and how far what she does select underdetermines the interpretations she gives is difficult to assess, even if Broughton and Nails are correct in the particular criticisms they make.

25 M. Moody-Adams, 'Gender and the Complexity of Moral Voices' in C. Card (ed) *Feminist Ethics* (Lawrence, Kansas: University of Kansas Press, 1991), p. 204.
26 See J. M. Broughton, 'Women's Rationality and Men's Virtues: A Critique of Gender Dualism in Gilligan's Theory of Moral Development', *Social Research*, vol. 50, 1983, pp. 603–6.
27 See D. Nails, 'Social-Scientific Sexism: Gilligan's Mismeasure of Man', *Social Research*, vol. 50, 1983, pp. 646–53.

2 Is it a person's sense of self that explains how she reasons on moral matters?

Even if Gilligan has correctly associated an ethics of care with women, and an ethics of rights with men, it is not obvious that the fact many women reason according to an ethics of care and many men according to an ethics of rights can be explained in terms of their different senses of self.

Some have argued that if Gilligan's findings are correct, the best explanation of them is to be found in the fact that men and women are forced, by structural factors, to perform different roles that require the exercise and development of contrasting ways of thinking, e.g. women become mothers and wives and develop an ethics of care.[28] But this could not by itself account for why girls reason according to an ethics of care (if indeed they do) and also does not explain why women come to *want* to mother.[29] The different kind of activities in which women are forced to engage surely plays some role in explaining their different foci of moral concern but it does not exhaust that explanation.

A number of writers have suggested that we see women's acceptance of an ethics of care as a function of the fact that they have been, and continue to be, oppressed. An ethics of care is a way that women have of coping with their subordinate position in relation to men. Bill Puka, for example, has reconstructed the various different stages of moral development distinguished by Gilligan as a set of 'coping strategies' employed by women in the face of sexist institutions, practices and individuals.[30] (In this light, even a qualified celebration of many women's acceptance of an ethics of care may seem to reveal a misunderstanding of the mechanisms which lead them to do so.)

No doubt sometimes women's acceptance of an ethics of care (and indeed the other stages Gilligan identifies) is simply a way of coping with sexism. But Chodorow's research on psychosexual development suggests that the rudimentary gender identity women acquire, and the subsequent full gender identity or identities into which it is

---

[28] See Nicholson, 'Women, Morality and History'; Grimshaw, *Feminist Philosophers*, pp. 201–2.

[29] See part I, section 4 of this appendix.

[30] B. Puka, 'The Liberation of Caring; A Different Voice for Gilligan's "Different Voice"', *Hypatia*, vol. 5, 1990, pp. 58–82. Cf. C. Card, 'Women's Voices and Ethical Ideals: Must We Mean What We Say?', *Ethics*, vol. 99, 1988, p. 128.

transformed by later experiences, disposes many women to reason according to an ethics of care. So it is plausible to think that many women who reason in accordance with an ethics of care do so because they have a sense of self in terms of connection. Even if women were not inclined because of their psychosexual development to embrace an ethics of care, they would have a motive for doing so in so far as an ethics of care does provide an effective means of coping with sexism; so the acceptance of an ethics of care may well be over-determined.

Bibliography

Allison, L. *Right Principles: A Conservative Philosophy of Politics* (Oxford: Blackwell, 1984)

Aristotle *The Nicomachean Ethics*, trans. W. D. Ross (Oxford: Oxford University Press, 1980)

Auerbach, J., L. Blum, V. Smith and C. Williams 'Commentary on Gilligan's *In a Different Voice*', *Feminist Studies*, vol. 11, 1985, 149–61

Ayer, A. J. *Language, Truth and Logic* second edition (New York: Dover, 1952)

Baier, A. 'What Do Women Want in a Moral Theory?', *Nous*, vol. 19, 1985, 53–65

Ball, T. *Transforming Political Discourse* (Oxford: Blackwell, 1988)

Barry, B. 'The Obscurities of Power', *Government and Opposition*, vol. 10, 1975, 250–4

Baumrind, D. 'Sex Differences in Moral Reasoning: Response to Walker's (1984) Conclusion That There Are None', *Child Development*, vol. 57, 1986, 511–21

Bentham, J. *A Comment on the Commentaries and A Fragment on Government*, ed. J. H. Burns and H. L. A. Hart (London: Athlone, 1977)

Blackburn, S. 'Error and the Phenomenology of Value' in T. Honderich (ed.) *Morality and Objectivity: A Tribute to J. L. Mackie* (London: Routledge and Kegan Paul, 1985)

Boyd, R. 'How to Be a Moral Realist', in G. Sayre-McCord (ed.) *Essays on Moral Realism* (Ithaca, NY: Cornell University Press, 1989)

Brink, D. *Moral Realism and the Foundations of Ethics* (Cambridge: Cambridge University Press, 1989)

Broughton, J. M. 'Women's Rationality and Men's Virtues: A Critique of Gender Dualism in Gilligan's Theory of Moral Development', *Social Research*, vol. 50, 1983, 597–642

Buchanan, A. E. *Marx and Justice: The Radical Critique of Liberalism* (London: Methuen, 1982)

Card, C. 'Women's Voices and Ethical Ideals: Must We Mean What We Say?', *Ethics*, vol. 99, 1988, 125–35

Chodorow, N. *The Reproduction of Mothering: Psychoanalysis and the Sociology of*

Gender (Berkeley and Los Angeles, CA: University of California Press, 1978)

Feminism and Psychoanalytic Theory (Cambridge: Polity, 1989)

Cohen, G. A. *Karl Marx's Theory of History: A Defence* (Princeton, NJ: Princeton University Press, 1978)

History, Labour and Freedom: Themes from Marx (Oxford: Oxford University Press, 1988)

Connolly, W. *The Terms of Political Discourse* second edition (Oxford: Martin Robertson, 1983)

Copi, I. *Introduction to Logic*, sixth edition (London: Collier-MacMillan, 1982)

Dancy, J. 'Ethical Particularism and Morally Relevant Properties', *Mind*, vol. 92, 1983, 530–47

An Introduction to Contemporary Epistemology (Oxford: Blackwell, 1986)

Dant, T. *Knowledge, Ideology and Discourse: A Sociological Perspective* (London: Routledge, 1991)

Davidson, D. 'Actions, Reasons and Causes' in his *Essays on Actions and Events* (Oxford: Oxford University Press, 1980)

'On the Very Idea of a Conceptual Scheme' in his *Inquiries into Truth and Interpretation* (Oxford: Oxford University Press, 1984)

Delphy, C. *Close to Home: A Materialist Understanding of Women's Oppression* (London: Hutchinson, 1984)

Devitt, M. and K. Sterelny *Language and Reality: An Introduction to the Philosophy of Language* (Oxford: Blackwell, 1987)

Dworkin, R. *Law's Empire* (London: Fontana, 1986)

Elshtain, J. 'Symmetry and Soporifics: A Critique of Feminist Accounts of Gender Development' in B. Richards (ed.) *Capitalism and Infancy: Essays on Psychoanalysis and Politics* (London: Free Association Books, 1984)

Elster, J. *Making Sense of Marx* (Cambridge: Cambridge University Press, 1985)

Farganis, S. *The Social Reconstruction of the Feminine Character* (Totowa, NJ: Rowman and Littlefield, 1986)

Feinberg, J. *The Moral Limits of the Criminal Law, vol. 1: Harm to Others* (New York: Oxford University Press, 1984)

Ferguson, A. and N. Folbre 'The Unhappy Marriage of Patriarchy and Capitalism' in L. Sargent (ed.) *Women and Revolution: A Discussion of the Unhappy Marriage of Marxism and Feminism* (Boston, MA: South End Press, 1981)

Fraser, N. and L. J. Nicholson 'Social Criticism without Philosophy: An Encounter between Feminism and Postmodernism' in L. J. Nicholson (ed.) *Feminism/Postmodernism* (London: Routledge, 1990)

Freud, S. *The Standard Edition of the Complete Works of Sigmund Freud*, trans. and ed. J. Strachey (London: Hogarth Press, 1955)

Friedman, M. 'Beyond Caring: The De-Moralization of Gender' in M. Hanen and K. Nielsen (eds.) *Science, Morality and Feminist Theory, Canadian Journal of Philosophy*, suppl. vol. 13, 1987, 87–110

Gallie, W. B. 'Essentially Contested Concepts', *Proceedings of the Aristotelian Society*, vol. 56, 1955–56, 167–98

Philosophy and the Historical Understanding (London: Chatto and Windus, 1964)

Gellner, E. 'The Concept of a Story', *Ratio*, vol. 19, 1967, 49–66

Geras, N. 'Seven Types of Obloquy: Travesties of Marxism' in R. Miliband, L. Panitch and J. Saville (eds.) *Socialist Register*, (London: Merlin Press, 1990)

Gilligan, C. *In a Different Voice: Psychological Theory and Women's Development* (Cambridge, MA: Harvard University Press, 1982)

'Moral Orientation and Moral Development' in E. Kittay and D. Meyers (eds.) *Women and Moral Theory* (Totowa, NJ: Rowman and Littlefield, 1987)

Goldman, A. 'A Causal Theory of Knowing', *Journal of Philosophy*, vol. 64, 1967, 355–72

Graham, K. 'Regulative Political Theory: Language, Norms and Ideology', *Political Studies*, vol. 33, 1985, 19–37

Gray, J. 'On the Contestability of Social and Political Concepts', *Political Theory*, vol. 5, 1977, 331–48

'On Liberty, Liberalism and Essential Contestability', *British Journal of Political Science*, vol. 8, 1978, 385–402

'Political Power, Social Theory and Essential Contestability' in D. Miller and L. Siedentop (eds.) *The Nature of Political Theory* (Oxford: Oxford University Press, 1983)

Grimshaw, J. *Feminist Philosophers: Women's Perspectives on Philosophical Traditions* (Brighton, Sussex: Wheatsheaf Books Ltd, 1986)

'Masculinity, Femininity and Mothering', Hull Centre for Gender Studies, occasional paper no. 3

Gutmann, A. and D. Thompson 'Moral Conflict and Political Consensus', *Ethics*, vol. 101, 1990, 64–88

Habermas, J. 'Towards a Theory of Communicative Competence', *Inquiry*, vol. 13, 1970, 360–75

Legitimation Crisis (London: Heinemann, 1976)

Hampshire, S. *Thought and Action* (London: Chatto and Windus, 1959)

Hanson, N. *Patterns of Discovery: An Inquiry into the Conceptual Foundations of Science* (Cambridge: Cambridge University Press, 1958)

Harding, S. 'What is the Real Material Base of Patriarchy and Capital?' in L. Sargent (ed.) *Women and Revolution: A Discussion of the Unhappy Marriage of Marxism and Feminism* (Boston, MA: South End Press, 1981)

Hare, R. M. *Freedom and Reason* (Oxford: Oxford University Press, 1963)

'The Argument from Received Opinion' in his *Essays on Philosophical Method* (London: Macmillan, 1971)

'Rawls' Theory of Justice' in N. Daniels (ed.) *Reading Rawls: Critical Studies on Rawls's Theory of Justice* (Oxford: Blackwell, 1975)

Moral Thinking: Its Levels, Method and Point (Oxford: Oxford University Press, 1981)

Harman, G. *The Nature of Morality: An Introduction to Ethics* (New York: Oxford University Press, 1977)

Harris, J. 'The Marxist Conception of Violence', *Philosophy and Public Affairs*, vol. 3, 1974, 192–220

Hartmann, H. 'The Unhappy Marriage of Marxism and Feminism: Toward a More Progressive Union' in L. Sargent (ed.) *Women and Revolution: A Discussion of the Unhappy Marriage of Marxism and Feminism* (Boston, MA: South End Press, 1981)

Hobbes, T. *Leviathan*, ed. C. B. Macpherson (Harmondsworth, Middlesex: Penguin, 1968)

Hurley, S. *Natural Reasons: Persons and Polity* (Oxford: Oxford University Press, 1989)

Keat, R. *The Politics of Social Theory* (Oxford: Blackwell, 1981)

Kenyon, J. 'Doubts about the Concept of Reason', *Proceedings of the Aristotelian Society*, suppl. vol. 59, 1985, 249–67

Kerber, L. K. *et al.* 'On *In a Different Voice*: An Interdisciplinary Forum', *Signs: Journal of Women in Culture and Society*, vol. 11, 1986, 304–33

Kovesi, J. *Moral Notions* (London: Routledge and Kegan Paul, 1967)

Kripke, S. *Naming and Necessity* (Cambridge, MA: Harvard University Press, 1980)

Wittgenstein on Rules and Private Language (Cambridge, MA: Harvard University Press, 1982)

Kuhn, T. *The Structure of Scientific Revolutions* second edition (Chicago, IL: University of Chicago Press, 1970)

'Objectivity, Value Judgement, and Theory Choice' in his *The Essential Tension* (Chicago, IL: University of Chicago Press, 1977)

Kymlicka, W. *Contemporary Political Philosophy: An Introduction* (Oxford: Oxford University Press, 1990)

Larmore, C. *Patterns of Moral Complexity* (Cambridge: Cambridge University Press, 1987)

Leonard, P. *Personality and Ideology: Towards a Materialist Understanding of the Individual* (London: Macmillan, 1984)

Locke, J. *An Essay Concerning Human Understanding* vols. I and II (New York: Dover, 1959)

Lorber, J., R. Laub Coser, A. S. Rossi and N. Chodorow 'On *The Reproduction of Mothering*: A Methodological Debate', *Signs: Journal of Women in Culture and Society*, vol. 6, 1981, 500–14

Lovibond, S. *Realism and Imagination in Ethics* (Oxford: Blackwell, 1983)

Lukes, S. *Power: A Radical View* (London: Macmillan, 1974)

'Relativism: Cognitive and Moral', *Proceedings of the Aristotelian Society*, suppl. vol. 48, 1974, 165–89

Marxism and Morality (Oxford: Oxford University Press, 1985)
Moral Conflict and Politics (Oxford: Oxford University Press, 1991)
MacIntyre, A. 'The Essential Contestability of Some Social Concepts',
  Ethics, vol. 84, 1973, 1–9
After Virtue: A Study in Moral Theory (Notre Dame, IN: University of
  Notre Dame Press, 1981)
Whose Justice? Which Rationality? (London: Duckworth, 1988)
Mackie, J. L. *Ethics: Inventing Right and Wrong* (Harmondsworth, Middle-
  sex: Penguin, 1977)
Macpherson, C. B. *The Real World of Democracy* (Oxford: Oxford University
  Press, 1966)
McDowell, J. 'Are Moral Requirements Hypothetical Imperatives?', *Pro-
  ceedings of the Aristotelian Society*, suppl. vol. 52, 1978, 13–29
'Virtue and Reason', *The Monist*, vol. 62, 1979, 331–50
'Non-Cognitivism and Rule Following', in C. Leich and S. Holtzmann
  (eds.) *Wittgenstein: To Follow a Rule* (London: Routledge, 1981)
'Wittgenstein on Following a Rule', *Synthese*, vol. 58, 1984, 325–63
'Values and Secondary Qualities', in T. Honderich (ed.) *Morality and
  Objectivity: A Tribute to J. L. Mackie* (London: Routledge, 1985)
McGinn, C. *The Subjective View* (Oxford: Oxford University Press, 1983)
McNaughton, D. *Moral Vision: An Introduction to Ethics* (Oxford: Blackwell,
  1988)
Mannheim, K. *Ideology and Utopia* (London: Routledge, 1991)
Marsilius of Padua *Defensor Pacis*, translated with an introduction by
  A. Gewirth (Toronto: University of Toronto Press, 1980)
Marx, K. and F. Engels *Selected Works*, vols. I and II (London: Lawrence
  and Wishart, 1951)
Complete Works, vol. V (London: Lawrence and Wishart, 1976)
Mason, A. 'Locke on Disagreement over the Use of Moral and Political
  Terms', *The Locke Newsletter*, vol. 20, 1989, 63–75
'On Explaining Political Disagreement: the Notion of an Essentially
  Contested Concept', *Inquiry*, vol. 33, 1990, 81–98
'Gilligan's Conception of Moral Maturity', *Journal for the Theory of Social
  Behaviour*, vol. 20, 1990, 167–79
'Nozick on Self-Esteem', *Journal of Applied Philosophy*, vol. 7, 1990, 91–8
'Politics and the State', *Political Studies*, vol. 38, 1990, 575–87
'MacIntyre on Liberalism and its Critics: Tradition, Incommensurabi-
  lity and Disagreement' in J. Horton and S. Mendus (eds.) *After
  MacIntyre* (Cambridge: Polity, forthcoming)
Mill, J. S. *On Liberty* (New York: Bobbs-Merrill, 1956)
Miller, D. *Social Justice* (Oxford: Oxford University Press, 1976)
'Constraints on Freedom', *Ethics*, vol. 94, 1983, 66–86.
'Linguistic Philosophy and Political Theory' in D. Miller and L. Sieden-
  top (eds.) *The Nature of Political Theory* (Oxford: Oxford University
  Press, 1983)

'Reply to Oppenheim', *Ethics*, vol. 95, 1985, 310–14
'Altruism and the Welfare State' in J. D. Moon (ed.) *Responsibility, Rights and Welfare* (Boulder, CO and London: Westview Press, 1988)
Miller, R. *Analyzing Marx: Morality, Power and History* (Princeton, NJ: Princeton University Press, 1984)
Milligan, D. E. *Reasoning and the Explanation of Actions* (Brighton, Sussex: Harvester, 1980)
Mitchell, J. and J. Rose (eds.) *Feminine Sexuality: Jacques Lacan and the Ecole Freudienne* (London: Macmillan, 1982)
Moi, T. 'Patriarchal Thought and the Drive for Knowledge' in T. Brennan (ed.) *Between Feminism and Psychoanalysis* (London: Routledge, 1989)
Moody-Adams, M. 'Gender and the Complexity of Moral Voices', in C. Card (ed.) *Feminist Ethics* (Lawrence, Kansas: University of Kansas Press, 1991)
Nagel, T. 'Moral Conflict and Political Legitimacy', *Philosophy and Public Affairs*, vol. 16, 1987, 215–40
Nails, D. 'Social-Scientific Sexism: Gilligan's Mismeasure of Man', *Social Research*, vol. 50, 1983, 643–64
Newton-Smith, W. H. *The Rationality of Science* (London: Routledge and Kegan Paul, 1981)
Nicholson, L. J. 'Women, Morality and History', *Social Research*, vol. 50, 1983, 514–36
Nozick, R. *Anarchy, State and Utopia* (Oxford: Blackwell, 1974)
Philosophical Explanations (Oxford: Oxford University Press, 1981)
O'Neill, O. (formerly Nell) *Acting on Principle: An Essay on Kantian Ethics* (New York: Columbia University Press, 1975)
Constructions of Reason: Explorations of Kant's Practical Philosophy (Cambridge: Cambridge University Press, 1989)
Philp, M. *Godwin's Political Justice* (London: Duckworth, 1986)
Popper, K. *Conjectures and Refutations: The Growth of Scientific Knowledge* (London: Routledge and Kegan Paul, 1963)
Puka, B. 'The Liberation of Caring; A Different Voice for Gilligan's "Different Voice" ', *Hypatia*, vol. 5, 1990, 58–82
Putnam, H. 'The Meaning of "Meaning" ' in his *Collected Papers vol. II: Mind, Language and Reality* (Cambridge: Cambridge University Press, 1975)
Rawls, J. *A Theory of Justice* (Oxford: Oxford University Press, 1971)
'Kantian Constructivism in Moral Theory', *Journal of Philosophy*, vol. 77, 1980, 515–72
'Justice as Fairness: Political Not Metaphysical', *Philosophy and Public Affairs*, vol. 14, 1985, 223–51
'The Idea of an Overlapping Consensus', *Oxford Journal of Legal Studies*, vol. 7, 1987, 1–25
'The Priority of Right and Ideas of the Good', *Philosophy and Public Affairs*, vol. 17, 1988, 251–76

'The Domain of the Political and Overlapping Consensus', *New York University Law Review*, vol. 64, 1989, 233–55

Raz, J. *The Morality of Freedom* (Oxford, Oxford University Press, 1986)

Rich, A. 'Compulsory Heterosexuality and Lesbian Existence', in A. Snitow, C. Stansell and S. Thompson (eds.) *Desire: The Politics of Sexuality* (London: Virago, 1984)

Russell, B. 'Science and Ethics' in his *Religion and Science* (Oxford: Oxford University Press, 1935)

Sayers, J. 'Psychoanalysis and Personal Politics: A Response to Elizabeth Wilson', *Feminist Review*, vol. 10, 1982, 91–5

Sexual Contradictions: Psychology, Psychoanalysis and Feminism (London: Routledge, 1986)

Sayre-McCord, G. 'Moral Theory and Explanatory Impotence' in his (ed.) *Essays on Moral Realism* (Ithaca, NY: Cornell University Press, 1989)

Scheman, N. 'On Sympathy', *The Monist*, vol. 62, 1979, 320–30

'Individualism and the Objects of Psychology' in S. Harding and M. Hintikka (eds.) *Discovering Reality: Feminist Perspectives on Epistemology, Metaphysics, Methodology and the Philosophy of Science* (Dordrecht, Holland: Reidel, 1983)

Seabright, P. 'Objectivity, Disagreement, and Projectability', *Inquiry*, vol. 31, 1988, 25–51

Skillen, A. *Ruling Illusions: Philosophy and the Social Order* (Hassocks, Sussex: Harvester, 1977)

Spelman, E. *Inessential Woman: Problems of Exclusion in Feminist Thought* (London: Women's Press, 1990)

Stevenson, C. L. *Ethics and Language* (New Haven, CT: Yale University Press, 1944)

Stoller, R. J. *Sex and Gender: On the Development of Masculinity and Femininity* (London: Hogarth Press, 1968)

Sturgeon, N. 'Moral Explanations' in G. Sayre-McCord (ed.) *Essays on Moral Realism* (Ithaca, NY: Cornell University Press, 1989)

Swanton, C. 'On the "Essential Contestedness" of Political Concepts', *Ethics*, vol. 95, 1985, 811–27

Thompson, J. J. 'A Defence of Abortion', *Philosophy and Public Affairs*, vol. 1, 1971, 47–66

Walker, L. 'Sex Differences in the Development of Moral Reasoning: A Critical Review', *Child Development*, vol. 55, 1984, 677–91

Weitz, S. *Sex Roles: Biological, Psychological and Social Foundations* (New York: Oxford University Press, 1977)

Whitford, M. 'Representing Irigaray', in T. Brennan (ed.) *Between Feminism and Psychoanalysis* (London: Routledge, 1989)

Williams, B. A. O. *Problems of the Self* (Cambridge: Cambridge University Press, 1973)

Moral Luck: Philosophical Papers 1973–1980 (Cambridge: Cambridge University Press, 1981)

Ethics and the Limits of Philosophy (London: Fontana, 1985)
Wittgenstein, L. *Philosophical Investigations* third edition, trans. G. E. M.
    Anscombe (Oxford: Blackwell, 1967)
The Blue and Brown Books (Oxford: Blackwell, 1960)
Zettel, second edition, ed. G. E. M. Anscombe and G. H. von Wright,
    trans. G. E. M. Anscombe (Oxford: Blackwell, 1981)
Wong, D. 'Coping with Moral Conflict and Ambiguity', *Ethics*, vol. 102,
    1992, 763–78
Wright, C. 'Moral Values, Projection and Secondary Qualities', *Proceedings
    of the Aristotelian Society*, suppl. vol. 62, 1988, 1–26

Index